SELECTED WRITINGS
OF
JONATHAN EDWARDS

Edited, with an introduction, by
HAROLD P. SIMONSON
University of Washington

FREDERICK UNGAR PUBLISHING CO.
NEW YORK

MILESTONES
OF THOUGHT
in the History of Ideas

Fourth Printing, 1984

Printed in the United States of America

Library of Congress Catalog Card No. 78-1150-64

ISBN 0-8044-5349-7 (clothbound)
ISBN 0-8044-6132-5 (paperback)

To Martha

INTRODUCTION

Had Jonathan Edwards preached in America a hundred years earlier, he would have taken his place among those American Calvinists—Thomas Hooker, Thomas Shepard, John Cotton—who were not to be rivaled in New England for their rigorous thinking and massive erudition. In this company Edwards easily would have equaled their grandeur. He also would have had the security of knowing that, for all his intellectual scope, he was part of the dominant theological force of the time; moreover, that an undemocratic Holy Commonwealth would assure him a continuous pulpit. In short, had Edwards lived a century earlier, he would have been, so to speak, a man for his times.

Born in 1703, only three years before Benjamin Franklin, Edwards was destined to live in the "wrong" century. Not Calvinism but Arminianism and all manner of religious dissension and independence would prevail. The American eighteenth century would see, not a Holy Commonwealth, but a political democracy; it would be a century in which Yankee ingenuity rather than spiritual salvation would distinguish the successful man, a time when America's most brilliant theologian and philosopher—Jonathan Edwards himself—would discover that a powerful laity could send him away from his pulpit and church. He lived in a time preceding one of the world's greatest political and social revolutions, based upon assumptions about man's natural rights and free will. His final years he would spend in remote Stockbridge, Massachusetts, where among twelve white families and over 200 Indian families to whom he ministered,

he would write his *chef d'oeuvre*, a brilliant treatise re-
pudiating nearly every eighteenth-century assumption
about both man and God. Destined to fail in the cause
of American Calvinism, he nevertheless would win a
place among the greatest American thinkers. The extent
to which the victory can be attributed to his defeat con-
stitutes his own peculiar enigma.

Throughout his life Edwards honed his mind on controversy and opposition. An easier style would have required that he merely follow in the footsteps of his
grandfather, Solomon Stoddard, whom he succeeded in
the Northampton pulpit. But what Stoddard represented
became for Edwards the enemy force he would commit
his life to fight.

Before moving to Northampton in 1727, he held two
brief pastorates, one for eight months in New York City
and the other, for even less time, at Bolton, Connecticut.
He also served two years as tutor at Yale, his alma mater.
Even at this time his name was well known. His father,
Timothy Edwards, had been preaching in East Windsor,
Connecticut, since 1694, a post he would hold until his
death sixty-four years later in 1758. His mother, Esther
Stoddard Edwards, was the daughter of the renowned
Solomon Stoddard and Esther Warham Mather (Increase
Mather's widowed sister-in-law), herself the daughter
of John Warham, the first minister in the Connecticut
colony. Jonathan Edwards's marriage in 1727 to Sarah
Pierrepont further enhanced his familial distinction. His
wife was not only the daughter of James Pierrepont, first
minister in New Haven and one of the founders of Yale,
but the granddaughter (on her mother's side) of the
great Thomas Hooker. Important as these facts are, they
merely highlight Edwards's reputation, which was established at Northampton.

Here was the place where Stoddard had preached for
over half a century. Second only to Boston, this was a

highly desirable parish for young Edwards to accept; he had only to appropriate Stoddard's theology, to say nothing of his wide popularity, in order to secure his own early career. However, Edwards had already begun to suspect the subtle, and what he considered, the deleterious liberalism in Stoddard's preaching. Understandably deferential toward his grandfather during the two years they shared the pulpit, Edwards, at the age of twenty-six, was on his own after Stoddard's death in 1729; by 1731, he had begun to make that singular position unequivocal. The notable occasion was a sermon he delivered in Boston amid an impressive assemblage that included Harvard's elite. The sermon, "God Glorified in Man's Dependence," published a few weeks later for all New England to read, was not only Edwards's first published work but his open declaration that certain "schemes of divinity," like Stoddard's, which mitigated God's absolute sovereignty and man's absolute dependence, are "repugnant to the design and tenor of the gospel." Any doubt as to the theological direction the young man from Yale and Northampton would take in the future was settled in this sermon. Calvinism would once again have its advocate, belated but powerful, even majestic.

II

Stoddard's liberalism characterized most of New England during Edwards's time. It was a liberalism born at the Synod of 1662 when a plan was proposed and later ratified to allow children of church members, without evidence of religious conversion, to be baptized and thereby to gain full membership in the church. The implications of this Half-Way Covenant, as it was to be called, were far-reaching and profound. Religious conversion was no longer prerequisite to membership, and membership itself no longer marked the difference between those persons in the true fellowship and those still unconverted. Under Stoddard's influence, the rules for membership were relaxed even more, allowing admission to all persons who were baptized, whether or not they professed religious experience. Although such persons unable or unwilling to profess this experience were denied the sacrament of the Lord's Supper, Stoddard eventually made further concessions to allow even the unregenerate to take communion. Considering the social and sometimes political advantages of church membership in the community, it was hardly surprising that this concession attracted widespread approval. Whatever importance the covenant of grace once had had in man's justification and sainthood, the halfway privileges of the new covenant proved entirely sufficient even for those who initially had been denied communion. Between village prestige and the holy table, the choice offered no difficulty; and when later open to all, the sacred ordinance of communion offered no meaning.

Underlying this ecclesiastical liberalism lay an even deeper theological liberalism, stemming not from the Deists of the day but from a movement named for Jacob Arminius, a Dutch Calvinist, whose fame rests upon the bitter theological controversies he promulgated in early seventeenth-century Amsterdam and Leiden. For opposing the doctrine of predestination and its corollary article concerning the enslavement of the will, Arminius was condemned at the Calvinist Synod of Dort in 1619, ten years after his death. He and his followers had rejected the doctrine wherein God decrees both election and reprobation prior to Creation and allows the fall of man as a means of effecting His divine purpose. Such a doctrine, the Arminians insisted, represented God as creating man in order to have him to damn; and thus, they argued,

God becomes, as it were, the author of sin. Their opposition to this view, as they conceived it, was based on what they thought to be a fundamental contradiction between God's absolute sovereignty and man's self-determination, between God's foreknowledge and man's free will. Unable to reconcile the two, they were satisfied to settle for a doctrine of universal redemption based upon man's willful acceptance of election. Again, the implications were profound.

Coming under Arminian attack were the central doctrines of reformed theology: God's sovereignty, man's innate sinfulness, unconditional election, and irresistible grace. Too severe for the new liberalism, these doctrines underwent subtle modification until, through the preaching of Daniel Whitby and John Taylor in England, and Stoddard, Jonathan Mayhew, and Charles Chauncey in America, the Christian life was reduced to little more than piety and morality. The belief in God as First Cause yielded to a new affirmation proclaiming man as sufficient cause unto himself. Instead of religious conversion touching man's deepest self, liberal thinkers sought a rational understanding of nature and existence, and relentlessly claimed that orthodox doctrines made little contribution to such understanding. In short, by the third decade of the eighteenth century, Calvinism had lost its thunder. Its vision of human existence as a great and awesome drama was beclouded by the idea that nature is benign, man is reasonable, salvation is moral virtue and good works, and God is Universal Benevolence.

When Edwards took up his Northampton ministry, he knew that Calvinism had lost its vital claim among New Englanders. The onslaught of Arminianism, reinforced by the Half-Way Covenant, seemingly had done irreparable damage, even to the point that, before his death, Stoddard dared to suggest that, for ordination, ministers needed to profess no religious experience. Clearly, Calvinism spoke a different language from that of the new enlightenment, which was itself augmented by the compelling claims upon both the frontiersman to build settlements and the Boston merchant to make profits. What was even clearer to Edwards was that Protestantism had reached a crisis; the issues were as stark as those between God's sovereignty and human will, between religion as experience to be moved by and religion as abstraction simply to think about. Required now to contravene Stoddard, the community, and the enlightened spirit of the age, Edwards conceived his mission as nothing less than making sainthood in New England visible once again.

His 1731 sermon in Boston provided the explicit, unambiguous, absolute doctrinal basis. Redemption comes only through the arbitrary and free grace of God, whose absolute dominion is everlasting. All the good that man has "is in and through Christ." Furthermore, "it is God that gives us Christ"; "it is of him that we are in Christ Jesus." Deliverance from evil is an act of divine efficacy, never an act of human decision. In truth, the power displayed in human will is nothing less than the power of God. God is all; he is "infinitely above us." By himself man is nothing, and in all things he is dependent upon God.

Penetrating as this sermon was, none more firmly establishes Edwards's greatness than "A Divine and Supernatural Light," delivered in 1734. In it, Edwards describes the nature of religious experience. As if struggling to find words adequate to his thought, he declares that true religion obtains when a person experiences a *sense* of divine excellency, the work of redemption, and the revelation of God in scripture. The all-important word is "sense," perhaps the single word which summarizes Edwards's whole system of thought. To Edwards, religion was fundamentally experience, a regenerative experience leaving a person reoriented, changed, converted. Using the symbol of light, Edwards is careful to point out that this sense is not synonymous with personal conscience, physical sensation, artistic inspiration, or sentiment. Instead, the divine and supernatural light is apprehended as a true sense of God. A person "does not merely rationally believe that God is glorious, but he has a sense of the gloriousness of God in his heart." The difference between cognitive knowledge and true sense is that the "former rests only in the head . . . but the heart is concerned in the latter." In striking upon this basic distinction from which he never veered, Edwards said that religious conversion is neither piety nor good works but rather an overwhelming, intuitive, and immediate sense—a "sixth sense," as it were—of God's reality. Experiencing this sense was always to be exalted over reasoning about it; yet from this experience, Edwards asserted, reason itself would be "sanctified."

That this sermon shows Edwards as a mystic suggests a relationship between him and the later Transcendentalists. Emerson, for example, uses the term "reason" (as opposed to "undstanding") in the Kantian meaning as standing for the higher, intuitive faculty of the mind by which mind merges with ideal unity or spirit. Accordingly, "right reason" possesses a divine quality. Edwards, on the contrary, never identifies human reason with divine nature. Adam's fall once and for all established this distinctness. The light that "sanctifies" reason emanates from God, the Beheld, not from the beholder. A more helpful relationship to trace is that between Edwards and John Locke, whose *An Essay Concerning Human Understanding* Edwards read when he was only fourteen. According to Perry Miller, this occasion was "the central and decisive event in his intellectual life." It was from Locke that Edwards received his central notion that what the mind knows as ideas depends wholly upon sensation. The key, then, to his sermon, "The Divine and Supernatural Light," and to practically everything else Edwards wrote, is that experience, not reason and not propositional speculation, is the basis of religious living. Direct perception is the source of religious certainty.

By 1734 no one could doubt Edwards's intentions. In his attack upon the liberalism of Stoddard, he could hardly have been more explicit. Another fusillade sounded in Northampton with Edwards's "Justification by Faith Alone," a straightforward, uncompromising statement that demolished all illusions that, by doing good works, men are assured of God's approval. A covenant of works leads to pride and self-righteousness and is "fatal and ruinous to the souls of men." The only covenant, or contract, between God and man is that of grace; only through this instrumentality are men freed from sin and made truly righteous or justified. Not works but faith actualizes grace. Yet not faith, either. Edwards argued that, despite our faith, God is under no obligation to act. At this point Edwards again is at his best, and again he utilizes the scientific thinking of his day. We are indebted to Perry Miller for clarifying the extent to which Edwards utilized the ideas of Sir Isaac Newton to explain that faith does not work an effect "but is part of a sequence within a system of coherence" (Miller). Newtonian physics presupposes cause and effect but also hypothesizes that the effect is what it is without its being determined by a cause. In short, physics is something more than sequence or mechanism and, by analogy, justification or salvation (effect) is something more than man's faith (cause). Whatever this power is which causes atoms to cohere in sequence is not, said Newtonians, inherent in the atoms. Gravity, they said, is not synonymous with mass or solidity. What the cause of gravity or of the coherence of atoms is, Newton did not or could not say. Edwards, however, pursued the quest to the conclusion that, as gravity inheres in matter, so God inheres in gravity; and, in consequence, God inheres in all things. All things are in God. No matter is merely matter. God gives being and oneness to all substance. Again, by analogy, man is not justified because he has faith, but he has faith because he is first justified through God's arbitrary grace. Man's goodness is not prior but posterior to God's grace. When Edwards declares that God is sovereign, he means just that. In God is coherence.

Held within this conclusion is the doctrine of predestination. Severe though it is (Edwards rarely viewed life as anything but severe), this doctrine fits into place within the ultimate premise establishing God's foreknowledge and authority. That God judges is consistent with his sovereignty to judge. However harsh the judgments, they are part of a supreme coherence.

III

Abhorrent as Edwards's ideas were to New England liberals, he soon was to have an astounding, unforgettable effect. More than a defender of Calvinist orthodoxy, Edwards became the leader, the new champion, preaching a gospel of religious conversion. The nature of Edwards's success was that he conjoined word and experience. However austere the doctrine, he transformed it into a religious experience for his auditors. He was satisfied with nothing less than the immediate action of the Divine Spirit upon their souls. Despite Arminian heresies that had filtered into the Northampton congregation, Edwards saw his parish as the center of revivalism that for a time extended throughout most of New England. Biographer Ola Winslow suggests that these few years were for Edwards "the happiest time in all his ministry."

During this brief time, the Great Awakening triumphed over schism and discord.

Everyone in Northampton talked religion. Many testified about their experience of conversion. Aware that religious feelings were astir, Edwards wrote a curious pamphlet in the form of a letter to Benjamin Colman of Boston, published as "A Faithful Narrative of the Surprising Work of God" and documented with case studies of parishioners who had experienced the power of God even in Northampton. In his "Personal Narrative," Edwards later tells of his own religious awakening; now, in 1736, he told of the same phenomenon among the people to whom he had been ordained to minister. Unfortunately, the account emphasized the bizarre aspects of conversion, a mistake for which Edwards would pay heavily. For it was finally by its excesses that the Great Awakening collapsed. In 1737, however, Edwards approached the pinnacle of his public success; a new church built by his parishioners and formally dedicated on Christmas Day seemed symbolic.

George Whitefield's arrival in 1740 proved climactic. Into a region already spiritually quickened came this English evangelist, famous for his oratorical gifts and open-air preaching. During a tour lasting slightly more than one month, he set Edwards's country spiritually on fire. First in Boston, then in Northampton, Philadelphia, and back in Boston, throngs of people marveled at his style—his voice was said to be audible for several village blocks—and a good number succumbed to his power. In unbelievable contrast to the solemn, carefully written, New England sermon, Whitefield's preaching crackled with spontaneous drama. More by his verbal than intellectual mastery, he left his audiences deeply shaken and forever anxious about the eternal punishment God brings to the unredeemed. After his departure, revivals spread all over New England. But no single revival sermon became more famous than that which Edwards preached in Enfield on July 8, 1741. It is no exaggeration to say that this is the most famous sermon ever preached in America.

Always for Edwards was the problem of words. How could words be adequate to the thoughts and emotions of someone who himself had experienced the sense of God's omnipotence and who was ordained to serve as the means enabling others to know this same awesomeness? In this Enfield sermon—"Sinners in the Hands of an Angry God"—which Edwards was invited to deliver, he succeeded as perhaps no one else has so unforgettably done. This sermon is not the raving of a George White-field or that of countless later American evangelists whose stock was little more than anti-intellectual bombast. Great literature and great philosophy, this sermon provides the necessary balance to "A Divine and Super-natural Light." In the earlier sermon, he captures the sense of divine effulgence; in this one he peers into the blackness of death, the emptiness of non-being. The two sermons together reconstruct the divine and human antipodes, the total view. Specifically, the Enfield sermon depicts the human condition, as modern and as terrifying as that in Kierkegaard's *Fear and Trembling* or Picasso's "Guernica." Most important, as with any great artist, Edwards not only depicts this condition but does so in a way that, through him, we experience it.

What Edwards said at Enfield was what man has always known, namely, that everyone is subject to "sudden, unexpected destruction." Today's scientific madness makes this eschatological reality only a push-button away. But Edwards, of course, meant something more than physical death. He was pointing to a condition of human sin characterized by spiritual disintegration and inner chaos where, as Hawthorne later was to describe, no light but lurid hellfire glows. Like a spider dangling over the abyss of total non-beingness, man is stripped of all contrivances, defenses, deceits. He sees what he truly is. This is his day of doom, his moment of judgment. Nothing in American literature is more dreadfully apocalyptic than Edwards's vision of what sin means. Life's utter precariousness can at any moment bring man to spiritual annihilation, to a complete and everlasting alienation from the source of all goodness and love. To know this is to know hell. Only by passing "under a great change of heart" can he ever know anything else.

Persons acquainted with Edwards through this one sermon inevitably think of him as the legendary hellfire preacher. On the basis of having read some 500 sermons, Ola Winslow attempts to contradict the legend by explaining that the Enfield sermon is not typical. When Edwards was most himself, she asserts, "he was a quiet-spoken teacher." Even during the Great Awakening, his subject was more often the sweet harmony existing between Christ and the true Christian. Another student, Thomas H. Johnson, suggests that only a third of Edwards's sermons are disciplinary, and of this number only a few, like "Sinners in the Hands of an Angry God," are clearly imprecatory in their emphasis upon man's depravity and the horrors of hell. The largest number belong to the pastoral type: sermons like "The Excellency of Christ" and "The Peace Which Christ Gives His True Followers," which stress the beauty of religious life. Doctrinal sermons like "God Glorified in Man's Dependence" and "A Divine and Supernatural Light" form another category, and occasional sermons like the "Farewell Sermon," delivered for a special occasion, comprise still another group.

Yet it was "Sinners in the Hands of an Angry God" and other sermons as severe, in doctrine if not in tone, that made him the target for liberal clergy who sought to blame him for the excesses rampant in the Awakening.

Deeply concerned about the shrieking and deliriums accompanying conversion among some worshipers, Edwards separated "true signs" and "false signs" as he tirelessly explained these phenomena on the profound level of religious psychology. Such an effort was his sermon, "The Distinguishing Marks of a Work of the Spirit of God," delivered at Yale two months after his Enfield sermon. Expanded and published the following year as *Some Thoughts Concerning the Present Revival in New England*, this work lays the foundation for what was later to rank Edwards as America's first significant thinker in the psychology of religion. In these shorter pieces and then in his major work, *A Treatise Concerning Religious Affections*, published in 1746, he distinguishes between understanding and inclination. The former relates to reason—to perception, speculation, discernment, judgment. The latter relates to affections, to heart feeling. Religion is primarily an affair of the heart. Only as religion affects this level of consciousness, only as Christ becomes one's basis for action, can Christianity be meaningful.

This book presents what Edwards considered the subliminal ideal of religious experience. Deeply personal though it is, the book also provided the psychological and theological groundwork for the Great Awakening which, ironically, was in shambles by the time Edwards published his great work.

Leading the attack against Edwards was Charles Chauncey, minister of the prestigious First Church of Boston, whose sermons on "The Late Religious Commotions in New England Considered" and "Seasonable Thoughts on the State of Religion," both published in 1743 and widely read, summarized the case against Edwards and the whole revivalism. God's presence cannot be proved by experience; emotionalism accompanying conversion cannot be attributed to the Holy Spirit; at its best Christianity is always rational; Satan can delude man through sensation and imagination. Furthermore, the Half-Way Covenant remained an important issue, one Edwards chose to keep alive by his insistence that church membership as well as the Holy Sacrament be privileges only for those visible saints who professed their Christian faith as founded upon a definite, specific religious experience. From 1744 to 1748 Edwards did not administer the sacrament to a single Northampton parishioner. Other circumstances also caused unrest. George Whitefield's return in 1744 tended obliquely to solidify feeling against Edwards. As for Whitefield, both Harvard and Yale drew up resolutions denouncing him, and many ministers refused to have him in their pulpits. Increasingly the term "new light," designating Edwards's kind of theology, was used disparagingly, especially as such revivalists as Whitefield, Gilbert and William Tennent, James Davenport, and Samuel Buel resorted to all manner of outrageous novelty in their preaching. Additionally, Northampton citizens objected to the style of living Edwards's family enjoyed, although his income was meager to support his wife and eleven children. The so-called "bad book case" in 1744, involving the surreptitious circulation of a midwife's handbook and the tactless publicity Edwards gave to the incident, increased the subtle rift between pulpit and congregation.

By 1750 it was clear that the issue concerning admission to the Lord's Supper would bring about Edwards's dismissal. He had stated his position in *A Treatise Concerning Religious Affections*; he stated it again in 1749 in *A Humble Inquiry Concerning Qualifications for Communion*. Eloquent in his determination to retain the purity of the sacrament and, with equal resoluteness, to retain his own ecclesiastical authority, he nevertheless accepted the 230-to-23 vote for his dismissal. Ten days

later, on July 2, 1750, he preached his "Farewell Sermon."
With neither rancor nor sentimentality, he spoke about
the judgment all men face and, thereby, with great tact
and authority, he placed his congregation's recent judgment into an infinitely larger perspective. With uncanny
vision, it was as if in this sermon of defeat and farewell
he pronounced his own vindication.

IV

In the summer of 1751 Edwards started work in Stockbridge, a frontier settlement sixty miles to the west. Left
behind were the local controversies marking the twenty-
three years he had spent in what still remained Stoddard
country. Also left behind was his final Northampton
polemic, *Misinterpretations Corrected and Truth Vindi-
cated*, written before he left but not published until 1752.
What he now faced in Stockbridge, however, was hardly
the refuge he anticipated. One congregation consisted of
Mohawks and Houcatannocks who hated each other; the
other consisted of whites who refused to unify their support. In addition to his duties as minister to these people,
he was obliged to supervise a boarding school for Indian
boys. Difficulties were compounded by the constant
threat of Indian warfare and the necessity, on occasions,
to offer his house as a place of protection for townspeople.
Finally, these seven years saw his health weaken, each
successive winter inflicting more injurious fevers.

Yet he adjusted to Stockbridge; he owned his house
and several hundred acres of land, and he had his family
all around him. Most important, he wrote his great
philosophical works. With a great burst of energy, he
finished his monumental masterpiece, *Freedom of the
Will*, in only four months; it was published in 1754. In

this mighty defense of Calvinism, he constructed a stately and intricate argument to prove that, even though man is free to gratify his will, he is not free to determine what the will chooses. Prior to the human will is a greater cause, and thus the will has its being only within the sphere of divine determinism.

In *A History of the Work of Redemption,* the amplification of previous sermons, he structured a sweeping, apocalyptic view of history, not to be matched in American historiography. As with many of his Stockbridge works, this one was published posthumously, first in Edinburgh in 1774 and then twelve years later in this country. Another work in which he raises some of the same eschatological questions was *Dissertation on the End for Which God Created the World,* published in 1765. Still another substantial work, the product of his years at Stockbridge, was *The Great Christian Doctrine of Original Sin Defended,* published in 1758. As if for one final time, Edwards in this book depicted man in all his corruption. We are all children of Adam, he said. Our acts are not those of independent wills but rather expressions of an underlying nature that all men share. In Adam's fall we all fell, and thus, like Adam, we are damned to utter alienation. But, as with the sermon, "A Divine and Supernatural Light," which, as it were, balances with "Sinners in the Hands of an Angry God," so also *The Nature of True Virtue,* published in 1765, serves as a counterstatement to this somber work. Furthermore, his book on true virtue serves as a sequel to the earlier *Treatise on Religious Affections.* In both books, Edwards treats the beauty of religious contemplation and experience. True virtue, he explains, is "that consent, propensity, and union of heart to being in general, which is immediately exercised in a general good will . . . a union and consent with the great whole." As the essence of religion, true virtue consists in love of neighbor and God. Showing great reverence for existence, Edwards affirms that the only real existence is in man's unity with God, the ultimate harmony.

This supreme insight of Edwards presages what now can be quickly told. Late in 1757 he was voted in as the third president of Princeton University, then named New Jersey College. On January 8, 1758, he preached his farewell sermon at Stockbridge, and on February 16 he was formally inaugurated as president. On March 22, at the age of fifty-four, he died from complications stemming from a smallpox inoculation he had received a week earlier. Inoculated at the same time, his daughter, Esther, wife of Aaron Burr, died two weeks after her father, and in the autumn of the same year his widow, Sarah Edwards, died. All lie buried in the Princeton cemetery.

Through the years Jonathan Edwards's place in American intellectual history has remained secure. In recent decades, however, as Americans have begun to question assumptions about man's natural goodness and reasonableness, the figure of Edwards has taken on larger proportions. For the same reasons that Hawthorne, Melville, and Poe are being reread, Edwards's interpretation of Christian truths speaks more tellingly to our human condition than ever before. His kind of theology, once eclipsed by Protestant liberalism and frontier anti-intellectualism, is being heard again, not in American pulpits but in American novels, plays, and poems. Once again the Christian epic recounting man's innocence and subsequent disaster, his beginning and his end, provides the awesome background to what we read each day in newspaper headlines. We yet may realize that Edwards's vision corroborates our own.

NOTE ON THE TEXT

Throughout this edition the text is from *The Works of President Edwards*, 4 vols., New York, 1869.

SELECTED BIBLIOGRAPHY

The fullest bibliographies on Jonathan Edwards appear in Lewis Leary, *Articles on American Literature, 1900–1950*, Duke University Press, 1954; Robert E. Spiller, *et al.* (eds.), *Literary History of the United States*, III, New York, 1948, with Richard M. Ludwig, ed., Supplement, New York, 1959; and the annual bibliographies of *PMLA*.

Complete editions of Edwards's works are not easily accessible. Of particular importance are modern editions of separate works, most notably: Perry Miller, ed., *Images or Shadows of Divine Things*, Yale, 1948; Paul Ramsey, ed., *Freedom of the Will*, Yale, 1957; John E. Smith, ed., *Religious Affections*, Yale, 1959; Clyde A. Holbrook, ed., *The Great Doctrine of Original Sin Defended*, Yale, 1970. Also valuable as a one-volume edition of selected works, containing an introduction and annotated bibliography, is Clarence H. Faust and Thomas H. Johnson, *Jonathan Edwards*, New York, 1935, 1962.

The following six scholarly studies are especially recommended:

1. Alfred Owen Aldridge, *Jonathan Edwards*, New York, 1964.
2. Alexander V. G. Allen, *Jonathan Edwards*, Boston, 1889.
3. James Carse, *Jonathan Edwards and the Visibility of God*, New York, 1967.
4. Douglas J. Elwood, *The Philosophical Theology of Jonathan Edwards*, Columbia University Press, 1960.
5. Perry Miller, *Jonathan Edwards*, New York, 1949.
6. Ola Elizabeth Winslow, *Jonathan Edwards, 1703–1758*, New York: The Macmillan Company, 1940.

TABLE OF CONTENTS

PERSONAL NARRATIVE

. . . I had a variety of concerns and exercises about my soul from my childhood; but had two more remarkable seasons of awakening, before I met with that change by which I was brought to those new dispositions, and that new sense of things, that I have since had. The first time was when I was a boy, some years before I went to college, at a time of remarkable awakening in my father's congregation. I was then very much affected for many months, and concerned about the things of religion, and my soul's salvation; and was abundant in duties. I used to pray five times a day in secret, and to spend much time in religious talk with other boys; and used to meet with them to pray together. I experienced I know not what kind of delight in religion. My mind was much engaged in it, and had much self-righteous pleasure; and it was my delight to abound in religious duties. I with some of my school-mates joined together, and built a booth in a swamp, in a very retired spot, for a place of prayer. And besides, I had particular secret places of my own in the woods, where I used to retire by myself; and was from time to time much affected. My affections seemed to be lively and easily moved, and I seemed to be in my element when engaged in religious duties. And I am ready to think, many are deceived with such affections, and such a kind of delight as I then had in religion, and mistake it for grace.

But in process of time, my convictions and affections wore off; and I entirely lost all those affections and delights and left off secret prayer, at least as to any constant performance of it; and returned like a dog to his vomit,

27

and went on in the ways of sin. Indeed I was at times very uneasy, especially towards the latter part of my time at college; when it pleased God to seize me with a pleurisy, in which he brought me nigh to the grave, and shook me over the pit of hell. And yet, it was not long after my recovery, before I fell again into my old ways of sin. But God would not suffer me to go on with any quietness; I had great and violent inward struggles, till, after many conflicts with wicked inclinations, repeated resolutions, and bonds that I laid myself under by a kind of vows to God, I was brought wholly to break off all former wicked ways, and all ways of known outward sin; and to apply myself to seek salvation, and practice many religious duties; but without that kind of affection and delight which I had formerly experienced. My concern now wrought more by inward struggles and conflicts, and self-reflections. I made seeking my salvation the main business of my life. But yet, it seems to me I sought after a miserable manner; which has made me sometimes since to question, whether ever it issued in that which was saving; being ready to doubt, whether such miserable seeking ever succeeded. I was indeed brought to seek salvation in a manner that I never was before; I felt a spirit to part with all things in the world, for an interest in Christ. My concern continued and prevailed, with many exercising thoughts and inward struggles; but yet it never seemed to be proper to express that concern by the name of terror.

Sovereignty of God

From my childhood up, my mind had been full of objections against the doctrine of God's sovereignty, in choosing whom he would to eternal life, and rejecting whom he pleased; leaving them eternally to perish, and be everlastingly tormented in hell. It used to appear like a horrible doctrine to me. But I remember the time very well, when I seemed to be convinced, and fully satisfied, as to this sovereignty of God, and his justice in thus eternally disposing of men, according to his sovereign pleasure. But I never could give an account how, or by what means, I was thus convinced, not in the least imagining at the time, nor a long time after, that there was any extraordinary influence of God's Spirit in it; but only that now I saw further, and my reason apprehended the justice and reasonableness of it. However, my mind rested in it; and it put an end to all those cavils and objections. And there has been a wonderful alteration in my mind, with respect to the doctrine of God's sovereignty, from that day to this; so that I scarce ever have found so much as the rising of an objection against it, in the most absolute sense, in God's showing mercy to whom he will show mercy, and hardening whom he will. God's absolute sovereignty and justice, with respect to salvation and damnation, is what my mind seems to rest assured of, as much as of any thing that I see with my eyes; at least it is so at times. But I have often, since that first conviction, had quite another kind of sense of God's sovereignty that I had then. I have often since had not only a conviction, but a delightful conviction. The doctrine has very often appeared exceeding pleasant, bright, and sweet. Absolute sovereignty is what I love to ascribe to God. But my first conviction was not so.

The first instance that I remember of that sort of inward, sweet delight in God and divine things that I have lived much in since, was on reading those words, 1 Tim. i. 17, "Now unto the King eternal, immortal, invisible, the only wise God, be honor and glory forever and ever, Amen." As I read the words, there came into my soul, and was as it were diffused through it, a sense of the glory of the Divine Being; a new sense, quite different from any thing I ever experienced before. Never any words of Scripture seemed to me as these words did.

I thought with myself, how excellent a Being that was, and how happy I should be, if I might enjoy that God, and be rapt up to him in heaven, and be as it were swallowed up in him forever! I kept saying, and as it were singing over these words of Scripture to myself; and went to pray to God that I might enjoy him, and prayed in a manner quite different from what I used to do; with a new sort of affection. But it never came into my thought, that there was any thing spiritual or of a saving nature, in this.

From about that time, I began to have a new kind of apprehensions and ideas of Christ, and the work of redemption, and the glorious way of salvation by him. An inward, sweet sense of these things, at times, came into my heart; and my soul was led away in pleasant views and contemplations of them. And my mind was greatly engaged to spend my time in reading and meditating on Christ, on the beauty and excellency of his person, and the lovely way of salvation by free grace in him. I found no books so delightful to me, as those that treated of these subjects. Those words, Cant. ii. 1, used to be abundantly with me, "I am the Rose of Sharon, and the Lily of the valleys." The words seemed to me sweetly to represent the loveliness and beauty of Jesus Christ. The whole book of Canticles used to be pleasant to me, and I used to be much in reading it, about that time; and found, from time to time, an inward sweetness, that would carry me away, in my contemplations. This I know not how to express otherwise, than by a calm, sweet abstraction of soul from all the concerns of this world; and sometimes a kind of vision, or fixed ideas and imaginations, of being alone in the mountains, or some solitary wilderness, far from all mankind, sweetly conversing with Christ, and rapt and swallowed up in God. The sense I had of divine things, would often of a sudden kindle up, as it were, a sweet burning in my heart; an ardor of soul that I know not how to express.

Growth of Spiritual Life

Not long after I first began to experience these things, I gave an account to my father of some things that had passed in my mind. I was pretty much affected by the discourse we had together; and when the discourse was ended, I walked abroad alone, in a solitary place in my father's pasture, for contemplation. And as I was walking there, and looking up on the sky and clouds, there came into my mind so sweet a sense of the glorious *majesty* and *grace* of God, that I know not how to express. I seemed to see them both in a sweet conjunction; majesty and meekness joined together; it was a sweet and gentle, and holy majesty; and also a majestic meekness; an awful sweetness; a high, and great, and holy gentleness.

After this my sense of divine things gradually increased, and became more and more lively, and had more of that inward sweetness. The appearance of every thing was altered; there seemed to be, as it were, a calm, sweet cast, or appearance of divine glory, in almost every thing. God's excellency, his wisdom, his purity and love, seemed to appear in every thing; in the sun, and moon, and stars; in the clouds and blue sky; in the grass, flowers, trees; in the water, and all nature; which used greatly to fix my mind. I often used to sit and view the moon for continuance; and in the day spent much time in viewing the clouds and sky, to behold the sweet glory of God in these things; in the mean time, singing forth, with a low voice, my contemplations of the Creator and Redeemer. And scarce any thing, among all the works of nature, was so sweet to me as thunder and lightning; formerly, nothing had been so terrible to me. Before, I used to be uncommonly terrified with thunder, and to be struck with terror when I saw a thunder storm rising; but now, on the contrary, it rejoiced me. I felt God, so to speak, at the first appearance of a thunder storm; and used to take the opportunity, at such times, to fix myself in order to view the clouds and see the lightnings play, and hear the majestic and awful voice of God's thunder, which oftentimes was exceedingly entertaining, leading me to sweet contemplations of my great and glorious God. While thus engaged, it always seemed natural to me to sing, or chant forth my meditations; or, to speak my thoughts in soliloquies with a singing voice.

I felt then great satisfaction, as to my good state; but that did not content me. I had vehement longings of soul after God and Christ, and after more holiness, wherewith my heart seemed to be full, and ready to break; which often brought to my mind the words of the Psalmist, Psal. cxix. 28, "My soul breaketh for the longing it hath." I often felt a mourning and lamenting in my heart, that I had not turned to God sooner, that I might have had more time to grow in grace. My mind was greatly fixed on divine things; almost perpetually in the contemplation of them. I spent most of my time in thinking of divine things, year after year; often walking alone in the woods, and solitary places, for meditation, soliloquy, and prayer, and converse with God; and it was always my manner at such times, to sing forth my contemplations. I was almost constantly in ejaculatory prayer, wherever I was. Prayer seemed to be natural to me, as the breath by which the inward burnings of my heart had vent. The delights which I now felt in the things of religion, were of an exceeding different kind from those before mentioned, that I had when a boy; and what I had then no more notion of, than one born blind has of pleasant and beautiful colors. They were of a more inward, pure, soul-animating and refreshing nature. Those former delights never reached the heart; and did not arise from any sight of the divine excellency of the things of God; or any taste of the soul-satisfying, and life-giving good there is in them.

My sense of divine things seemed gradually to increase,

until I went to preach at New-York, which was about a year and a half after they began; and while I was there I felt them, very sensibly, in a much higher degree than I had done before. My longings after God and holiness were much increased. Pure and humble, holy and heavenly Christianity, appeared exceedingly amiable to me. I felt a burning desire to be in every thing a complete Christian; and conformed to the blessed image of Christ; and that I might live, in all things, according to the pure, sweet, and blessed rules of the gospel. I had an eager thirsting after progress in these things; which put me upon pursuing and pressing after them. It was my continual strife day and night, and constant inquiry, how I should *be* more holy, and *live* more holily, and more becoming a child of God, and a disciple of Christ. I now sought an increase of grace and holiness, and a holy life, with much more earnestness than ever I sought grace before I had it. I used to be continually examining myself, and studying and contriving for likely ways and means, how I should live holily, with far greater diligence and earnestness, than ever I pursued any thing in my life; but yet with too great a dependence on my own strength; which afterwards proved a great damage to me. My experience had not then taught me, as it has done since, my extreme feebleness and impotence, every manner of way; and the bottomless depths of secret corruption and deceit there was in my heart. However, I went on with my eager pursuit after more holiness, and conformity to Christ.

The heaven I desired was a heaven of holiness; to be with God, and to spend my eternity in divine love, and holy communion with Christ. My mind was very much taken up with contemplations on heaven, and the enjoyments there; and living there in perfect holiness, humility, and love; and it used at that time to appear a great part of the happiness of heaven, that there the saints could express their love to Christ. It appeared to me a great clog and burden, that what I felt within, I could not express as I desired. The inward ardor of my soul seemed to be hindered and pent up, and could not freely flame out as it would. I used often to think, how in heaven this principle should freely and fully vent and express itself. Heaven appeared exceedingly delightful, as a world of love; and that all happiness consisted in living in pure, humble, heavenly, divine love.

I remember the thoughts I used then to have of holiness; and said sometimes to myself, "I do certainly know that I love holiness, such as the gospel prescribes." It appeared to me that there was nothing in it but what was ravishingly lovely; the highest beauty and amiableness— a *divine* beauty; far purer than any thing here upon earth; and that every thing else was like mire and defilement, in comparison of it.

Holiness, as I then wrote down some of my contemplations on it, appeared to me to be of a sweet, pleasant, charming, serene, calm nature; which brought an inexpressible purity, brightness, peacefulness and ravishment to the soul. In other words, that it made the soul like a field or garden of God, with all manner of pleasant flowers; all pleasant, delightful, and undisturbed; enjoying a sweet calm, and the gentle vivifying beams of the sun. The soul of a true Christian, as I then wrote my meditations, appeared like such a little white flower as we see in the spring of the year; low and humble on the ground, opening its bosom to receive the pleasant beams of the sun's glory; rejoicing as it were in a calm rapture; diffusing around a sweet fragrancy; standing peacefully and lovingly, in the midst of other flowers round about; all in like manner opening their bosoms, to drink in the light of the sun. There was no part of creature holiness, that I had so great a sense of its loveliness, as humility, brokenness of heart, and poverty of spirit; and there was nothing that I so earnestly longed for. My heart panted after this, to lie low before God, as in the dust; that I might be nothing, and that God might be ALL, that I might become as a little child.

While at New-York, I was sometimes much affected with reflections on my past life, considering how late it was before I began to be truly religious; and how wickedly I had lived till then; and once so as to weep abundantly, and for a considerable time together.

On *January* 12, 1723, I made a solemn dedication of myself to God, and wrote it down; giving up myself and all I had to God; to be for the future in no respect my own; to act as one that had no right to himself in any respect. And solemnly vowed to take God for my whole portion and felicity; looking on nothing else as any part of my happiness, nor acting as if it were; and his law for the constant rule of my obedience; engaging to fight with all my might, against the world, the flesh, and the devil, to the end of my life. But I have reason to be infinitely humbled, when I consider how much I have failed of answering my obligation.

I had then abundance of sweet religious conversation in the family where I lived, with Mr. John Smith and his pious mother. My heart was knit in affection to those in whom were appearances of true piety; and I could bear the thoughts of no other companions but such as were holy, and the disciples of the blessed Jesus. I had great longings for the advancement of Christ's kingdom in the world; and my secret prayer used to be, in great part, taken up in praying for it. If I heard the least hint of any thing that happened, in any part of the world, that appeared, in some respect or other, to have a favorable aspect on the interests of Christ's kingdom, my soul eagerly catched at it; and it would much animate and refresh me. I used to be eager to read public news letters, mainly for that end; to see if I could not find some news favorable to the interest of religion in the world.

I very frequently used to retire into a solitary place,

on the banks of Hudson's river, at some distance from the city, for contemplation on divine things, and secret converse with God; and had many sweet hours there. Sometimes Mr. Smith and I walked there together, to converse on the things of God; and our conversation used to turn much on the advancement of Christ's kingdom in the world, and the glorious things that God would accomplish for his church in the latter days. I had then, and at other times, the greatest delight in the holy Scriptures, of any book whatsoever. Oftentimes in reading it, every word seemed to touch my heart. I felt a harmony between something in my heart, and those sweet and powerful words. I seemed often to see so much light exhibited by every sentence, and such a refreshing food communicated, that I could not get along in reading; often dwelling long on one sentence, to see the wonders contained in it; and yet almost every sentence seemed to be full of wonders.

Further Reflections

I came away from New-York in the month of April, 1723, and had a most bitter parting with Madam Smith and her son. My heart seemed to sink within me at leaving the family and city, where I had enjoyed so many sweet and pleasant days. I went from New-York to Wethersfield, by water, and as I sailed away, I kept sight of the city as long as I could. However, that night, after this sorrowful parting, I was greatly comforted in God at Westchester, where we went ashore to lodge; and had a pleasant time of it all the voyage to Saybrook. It was sweet to me to think of meeting dear Christians in heaven, where we should never part more. At Saybrook we went ashore to lodge on Saturday, and there kept the Sabbath; where I had a sweet and refreshing season, walking alone in the fields.

After I came home to Windsor, I remained much in a

like frame of mind, as when at New-York; only sometimes I felt my heart ready to sink with the thoughts of my friends at New-York. My support was in contemplations on the heavenly state; as I find in my Diary of May 1, 1723. It was a comfort to think of that state, where there is fulness of joy; where reigns heavenly, calm, and delightful love, without alloy; where there are continually the dearest expressions of love; where is the enjoyment of the persons loved, without ever parting; where these persons who appear so lovely in this world, will really be inexpressibly more lovely and full of love to us. And how sweetly will the mutual lovers join together to sing the praises of God and the Lamb! How will it fill us with joy to think, that this enjoyment, these sweet exercises will never cease but will last to all eternity! I continued much in the same frame, in the general, as when at New-York, till I went to New Haven as tutor to the college; particularly once at Bolton, on a journey from Boston, while walking out alone in the fields. After I went to New Haven I sunk in religion; my mind being diverted from my eager pursuits after holiness, by some affairs that greatly perplexed and distracted my thoughts.

In September, 1725, I was taken ill at New Haven, and while endeavoring to go home to Windsor, was so ill at the North Village, that I could go no further; where I lay sick for about a quarter of a year. In this sickness God was pleased to visit me again with the sweet influences of his Spirit. My mind was greatly engaged there in divine, pleasant contemplations, and longings of soul. I observed that those who watched with me, would often be looking out wishfully for the morning; which brought to my mind those words of the Psalmist, and which my soul with delight made its own language, "My soul waiteth for the Lord, more than they that watch for the morning, I say, more than they that watch for the morning"; and when the light of day came in at the windows, it refreshed my soul from one morning to another. It seemed to be some image of the light of God's glory.

I remember, about that time, I used greatly to long for the conversion of some that I was concerned with; I could gladly honor them, and with delight be a servant to them, and lie at their feet, if they were but truly holy. But, some time after this, I was again greatly diverted in my mind with some temporal concerns that exceedingly took up my thoughts, greatly to the wounding of my soul; and went on through various exercises, that it would be tedious to relate, which gave me much more experience of my own heart, than ever I had before.

Since I came to this town [Northampton], I have often had sweet complacency in God, in views of his glorious perfections and the excellency of Jesus Christ. God has appeared to me a glorious and lovely Being, chiefly on the account of his holiness. The holiness of God has always appeared to me the most lovely of all his attributes. The doctrines of God's absolute sovereignty, and free grace, in showing mercy to whom he would show mercy; and man's absolute dependence on the operations of God's Holy Spirit, have very often appeared to me as sweet and glorious doctrines. These doctrines have been much my delight. God's sovereignty has ever appeared to me, great part of his glory. It has often been my delight to approach God, and adore him as a sovereign God, and ask sovereign mercy of him.

I have loved the doctrines of the gospel; they have been to my soul like green pastures. The gospel has seemed to me the richest treasure; the treasure that I have most desired, and longed that it might dwell richly in me. The way of salvation by Christ has appeared, in a general way, glorious and excellent, most pleasant and most beautiful. It has often seemed to me, that it would in a great measure spoil heaven, to receive it in any other way. That text has often been affecting and delightful to me, Isa. xxxii. 2, "A man shall be a hiding place from the wind, and a covert from the tempest," &c.

It has often appeared to me delightful, to be united to Christ; to have him for my head, and to be a member of his body; also to have Christ for my teacher and prophet. I very often think with sweetness, and longings, and pantings of soul, of being a little child, taking hold of Christ, to be led by him through the wilderness of this world. That text Matth. xviii. 3, has often been sweet to me, "Except ye be converted and become as little children," &c. I love to think of coming to Christ, to receive salvation of him, poor in spirit, and quite empty of self, humbly exalting him alone; cut off entirely from my own root, in order to grow into, and out of Christ; to have God in Christ to be all in all; and to live by faith on the Son of God, a life of humble, unfeigned confidence in him. That scripture has often been sweet to me, Psal. cxv. 1, "Not unto us, O Lord, not unto us, but unto thy name give glory, for thy mercy, and for thy truth's sake." And those words of Christ, Luke x. 21, "In that hour Jesus rejoiced in spirit, and said, I thank thee, O Father, Lord of heaven and earth, that thou hast hid these things from the wise and prudent, and hast revealed them unto babes; even so, Father, for so it seemed good in thy sight." That sovereignty of God which Christ rejoiced in, seemed to me worthy of such joy; and that rejoicing seemed to show the excellency of Christ, and of what spirit he was.

Sometimes, only mentioning a single word caused my heart to burn within me; or only seeing the name of Christ, or the name of some attribute of God. And God has appeared glorious to me, on account of the Trinity. It has made me have exalting thoughts of God, that he subsists in three persons; Father, Son, and Holy Ghost. The sweetest joys and delights I have experienced, have not been those that have arisen from a hope of my own good estate; but in a direct view of the glorious things of the gospel. When I enjoy this sweetness, it seems to carry me above the thoughts of my own estate; it seems at such times a loss that I cannot bear, to take off my eye from the glorious pleasant object I behold without me, to turn my eye in upon myself, and my own good estate.

My heart has been much on the advancement of Christ's kingdom in the world. The histories of the past advancement of Christ's kingdom have been sweet to me. When I have read histories of past ages, the pleasantest thing in all my reading has been, to read of the kingdom of Christ being promoted. And when I have expected, in my reading, to come to any such thing, I have rejoiced in the prospect, all the way as I read. And my mind has been much entertained and delighted with the Scripture promises and prophecies, which relate to the future glorious advancement of Christ's kingdom upon earth.

I have sometimes had a sense of the excellent fulness of Christ, and his meetness and suitableness as a Saviour; whereby he has appeared to me, far above all, the chief of ten thousands. His blood and atonement have appeared sweet, and his righteousness sweet; which was always accompanied with ardency of spirit; and inward strugglings and breathings, and groanings that cannot be uttered, to be emptied of myself, and swallowed up in Christ.

Once, as I rode out into the woods for my health, in 1737, having alighted from my horse in a retired place, as my manner commonly has been, to walk for divine contemplation and prayer, I had a view that for me was extraordinary, of the glory of the Son of God, as Mediator between God and man, and his wonderful, great, full, pure and sweet grace and love, and meek and gentle condescension. This grace that appeared so calm and sweet, appeared also great above the heavens. The person of Christ appeared ineffably excellent, with an excellency great enough to swallow up all thought and conception— which continued, as near as I can judge, about an hour; which kept me the greater part of the time in a flood of tears, and weeping aloud. I felt an ardency of soul to be what I know not otherwise how to express, emptied and annihilated; to lie in the dust, and to be full of Christ alone; to love him with a holy and pure love; to trust in him; to live upon him; to serve and follow him; and to be perfectly sanctified and made pure, with a divine and heavenly purity. I have, several other times, had views very much of the same nature, and which have had the same effects.

I have many times had a sense of the glory of the third person in the Trinity, in his office of sanctifier; in his holy operations, communicating divine light and life to the soul. God, in the communications of his Holy Spirit, has appeared as an infinite fountain of divine glory and sweetness; being full and sufficient to fill and satisfy the soul; pouring forth itself in sweet communications; like the sun in its glory, sweetly and pleasantly diffusing light and life. And I have sometimes had an affecting sense of the excellency of the word of God, as the word of life; as the light of life; a sweet, excellent, life-giving word; accompanied with a thirsting after that word, that it might dwell richly in my heart.

Often, since I lived in this town, I have had very affecting views of my own sinfulness and vileness; very frequently to such a degree as to hold me in a kind of loud weeping, sometimes for a considerable time together; so that I have often been forced to shut myself up. I have had a vastly greater sense of my own wickedness, and the badness of my heart, than ever I had before my conversion. It has often appeared to me, that if God should mark iniquity against me, I should appear the very worst of all mankind; of all that have been since the beginning of the world to this time; and that I should have by far the lowest place in the world to this time; and that I should have by far the lowest place in hell. When others, that have come to talk with me about their soul concerns, have expressed the sense they have had of their own wickedness, by saying that it seemed to them, that they were as bad as the devil himself; I thought their expressions seemed exceeding faint and feeble, to represent my wickedness.

My wickedness, as I am in myself, has long appeared to me perfectly ineffable, and swallowing up all thought and imagination; like an infinite deluge, or mountains over my head. I know not how to express better what my sins appear to me to be, than by heaping infinite upon infinite, and multiplying infinite by infinite. Very often, for these many years, these expressions are in my mind and in my mouth, "Infinite upon infinite—Infinite upon infinite!" When I look into my heart, and take a view of my wickedness, it looks like an abyss infinitely deeper than hell. And it appears to me, that were it not for free grace, exalted and raised up to the infinite height of all the fulness and glory of the great Jehovah, and the arm of his power and grace stretched forth in all the majesty of his power, and in all the glory of his sovereignty, I should appear sunk down in my sins below hell itself; far beyond the sight of every thing, but the eye of sovereign grace, that can pierce even down to such a depth. And yet it seems to me, that my conviction of sin is exceeding small, and faint; it is enough to amaze me, that I have no more sense of my sin. I know certainly, that I have very little sense of my sinfulness. When I have had turns of weeping for my sins, I thought I knew at the time that my repentance was nothing to my sin.

I have greatly longed of late for a broken heart, and to lie low before God; and, when I ask for humility, I cannot bear the thoughts of being no more humble than

other Christians. It seems to me, that though their degrees of humility may be suitable for them, yet it would
be a vile self-exaltation in me, not to be the lowest in
humility of all mankind. Others speak of their longing to
be "humbled in the dust"; that may be a proper expression for them, but I always think of myself, that I ought,
and it is an expression that has long been natural for me
to use in prayer, "to lie infinitely low before God." And
it is affecting to think, how ignorant I was, when a young
Christian, of the bottomless, infinite depths of wickedness, pride, hypocrisy and deceit, left in my heart.

I have a much greater sense of my universal, exceeding dependence on God's grace and strength, and mere
good pleasure, of late, than I used formerly to have; and
have experienced more of an abhorrence of my own
righteousness. The very thought of any joy arising in me,
on any consideration of my own amiableness, perform-
ances, or experiences, or any goodness of heart or life, is
nauseous and detestable to me. And yet I am greatly
afflicted with a proud and self-righteous spirit, much
more sensibly than I used to be formerly. I see that serpent rising and putting forth its head continually, every
where, all around me.

Though it seems to me, that, in some respects, I was a
far better Christian, for two or three years after my first
conversion, than I am now; and lived in a more constant
delight and pleasure; yet, of late years, I have had a more
full and constant sense of the absolute sovereignty of
God, and a delight in that sovereignty; and have had
more of a sense of the glory of Christ, as a Mediator
revealed in the gospel. On one Saturday night, in particular, I had such a discovery of the excellency of the
gospel above all other doctrines, that I could not but say
to myself, "This is my chosen light, my chosen doctrine";
and of Christ, "This is my chosen Prophet." It appeared
sweet, beyond all expression to follow Christ, and to be

taught, and enlightened, and instructed by him; to learn of him, and live to him. Another Saturday night (*January*, 1739) I had such a sense, how sweet and blessed a thing it was to walk in the way of duty; to do that which was right and meet to be done, and agreeable to the holy mind of God; that it caused me to break forth into a kind of loud weeping, which held me some time, so that I was forced to shut myself up, and fasten the doors. I could not but, as it were, cry out, "How happy are they which do that which is right in the sight of God! They are blessed indeed, they are the happy ones!" I had, at the same time, a very affecting sense, how meet and suitable it was that God should govern the world, and order all things according to his own pleasure; and I rejoiced in it, that God reigned, and that his will was done.

GOD GLORIFIED
IN MAN'S DEPENDENCE

I COR. i. 29–31—That no flesh should glory in his
presence. But of him are ye in Christ Jesus, who of God
is made unto us wisdom, and righteousness, and sanctification, and redemption; that according as is written.
He that glorieth, let him glory in the Lord.

Those Christians to whom the apostle directed this
epistle, dwelt in a part of the world where human wisdom
was in great repute; as the apostle observes in the 22d
verse of this chapter, "The Greeks seek after wisdom."
Corinth was not far from Athens, that had been for many
ages the most famous seat of philosophy and learning in
the world.

The apostle therefore observes to them, how that God,
by the gospel, destroyed and brought to naught their
human wisdom. The learned Grecians, and their great
philosophers, by all their wisdom did not know God:
they were not able to find out the truth in divine things.
But after they had done their utmost to no effect, it
pleased God at length to reveal himself by the gospel,
which they accounted foolishness. He "chose the foolish
things of the world to confound the wise, and the weak
things of the world to confound the things which are
mighty, and the base things of the world, and things
that are despised, yea, and things which are not, to bring
to nought the things that are." And the apostle informs
them why he thus did, in the verse of the text; *That no
flesh should glory in his presence,* &c.

In which words may be observed,

1. What God aims at in the disposition of things in the affair of redemption, viz., that man should not glory in himself, but alone in God; *That no flesh should glory in his presence,—that, according as it is written, He that glorieth, let him glory in the Lord.*

2. How this end is attained in the work of redemption, viz., by that absolute and immediate dependence which men have upon God in that work for their good. Inasmuch as,

FIRST. All the good that they have is in and through Christ; *He is made unto us wisdom, righteousness, sanctification, and redemption.* All the good of the fallen and redeemed creature is concerned in these four things, and cannot be better distributed than into them; but Christ is each of them to us, and we have none of them any otherwise than in him. *He is made of God unto us wisdom*: in him are all the proper good and true excellency of the understanding. Wisdom was a thing that the Greeks admired; but Christ is the true light of the world, it is through him alone that true wisdom is imparted to the mind. It is in and by Christ that we have righteousness: it is by being in him that we are justified, have our sins pardoned, and are received as righteous into God's favor. It is by Christ that we have sanctification: we have in him true excellency of heart as well as of understanding; and he is made unto us inherent, as well as imputed righteousness. It is by Christ that we have redemption, or actual deliverance from all misery, and the bestowment of all happiness and glory. Thus we have all our good by Christ, who is God.

SECONDLY. Another instance wherein our dependence on God for all our good appears, is this, That it is God that has given us Christ, that we might have these benefits through him; he *of God is made unto us wisdom, righteousness,* &c.

THIRDLY. It is of him that we are in Christ Jesus, and come to have an interest in him, and so do receive those blessings which he is made unto us. It is God that gives us faith whereby we close with Christ.

So that in this verse is shown our dependence on each person in the Trinity for all our good. We are dependent on Christ the Son of God, as he is our wisdom, righteousness, sanctification, and redemption. We are dependent on the Father, who has given us Christ, and made him to be these things to us. We are dependent on the Holy Ghost, for it is *of him that we are in Christ Jesus*; it is the Spirit of God that gives faith in him, whereby we receive him, and close with him.

Doctrine

"God is glorified in the work of redemption in this, that there appears in it so absolute and universal a dependence of the redeemed on him."

Here I propose to show, 1st, That there is an absolute and universal dependence of the redeemed on God for all their good. And 2dly, That God hereby is exalted and glorified in the work of redemption.

I. There is an absolute and universal dependence of the redeemed on God. The nature and contrivance of our redemption is such, that the redeemed are in every thing directly, immediately, and entirely dependent on God: they are dependent on him for all, and are dependent on him every way.

The several ways wherein the dependence of one being may be upon another for its good, and wherein the redeemed of Jesus Christ depend on God for all their good, are these, viz., that they have all their good of him, and that they have all through him, and that they have all in him: that he is the cause and original whence all their good comes, therein it is *of* him; and that he is the medium by which it is obtained and conveyed, therein they have it *through* him; and that he is that good itself that is given and conveyed, therein it is *in* him.

Now those that are redeemed by Jesus Christ do, in all these respects, very directly and entirely depend on God for their all.

FIRST. The redeemed have all their good of God; God is the great author of it; he is the first cause of it, and not only so, but he is the only proper cause.

It is of God that we have our Redeemer: it is God that has provided a Saviour for us. Jesus Christ is not only of God in his person, as he is the only begotten Son of God, but he is from God, as we are concerned in him, and in his office of Mediator: he is the gift of God to us: God chose and anointed him, appointed him his work, and sent him into the world.

And as it is God that gives, so it is God that accepts the Saviour. As it is God that provides and gives the Redeemer to buy salvation for us, so it is of God that salvation is bought: he gives the purchaser, and he affords the thing purchased.

It is of God that Christ becomes ours, that we are brought to him, and are united to him: it is of God that we receive faith to close with him, that we may have an interest in him. Eph. ii. 8, "For by grace ye are saved, through faith; and that not of yourselves, it is the gift of God." It is of God that we actually do receive all the benefits that Christ has purchased. It is God that pardons and justifies, and delivers from going down to hell, and it is his favor that the redeemed are received into, and are made the objects of, when they are justified. So it is God that delivers from the dominion of sin, and cleanses us from our filthiness, and changes us from our deformity. It is of God that the redeemed do receive all their true excellency, wisdom, and holiness; and that two ways, viz., as the Holy Ghost, by whom these things are immediately wrought, as from God, proceeds from him, and is sent by him; and also as the Holy Ghost himself is God, by whose operation and indwelling, the knowledge of divine things, and a holy disposition, and all grace, are conferred and upheld.

And though means are made use of in conferring grace on men's souls, yet it is of God that we have these means of grace, and it is God that makes them effectual. It is of God that we have the holy Scriptures; they are the word of God. It is of God that we have ordinances, and their efficacy depends on the immediate influence of the Spirit of God. The ministers of the gospel are sent of God, and all their sufficiency is of him. 2 Cor. iv. 7, "We have this treasure in earthen vessels, that the excellency of the power may be of God, and not of us." Their success depends entirely and absolutely on the immediate blessing and influence of God. The redeemed have all,

1. Of the grace of God. It was of mere grace that God gave us his only begotten Son. The grace is great in proportion to the dignity and excellency of what is given: the gift was infinitely precious, because it was a person infinitely worthy, a person of infinite glory; and also because it was a person infinitely near and dear to God. The grace is great in proportion to the benefit we have given us in him: the benefit is doubly infinite, in that in him we have deliverance from an infinite, because an eternal misery; and do also receive eternal joy and glory. The grace in bestowing this gift is great in proportion to our unworthiness to whom it is given; instead of deserving such a gift, we merited infinitely ill of God's hands. The grace is great according to the manner of giving, or in proportion to the humiliation and expense of the method and means by which way is made for our having the gift. He gave him to us dwelling amongst us; he gave him to us incarnate, or in our nature; he gave him to us in our nature, in the like infirmities, in which we have it in our fallen state, and which in us do accompany,

and are occasioned by the sinful corruption of our nature. He gave him to us in a low and afflicted state; and not only so, but he gave him to us slain, that he might be a feast for our souls.

The grace of God in bestowing this gift is most free. It was what God was under no obligation to bestow: he might have rejected fallen man, as he did the fallen angels. It was what we never did any thing to merit; it was given while we were yet enemies, and before we had so much as repented. It was from the love of God that saw no excellency in us to attract it; and it was without expectation of ever being requited for it.

And it is from mere grace that the benefits of Christ are applied to such and such particular persons. Those that are called and sanctified are to attribute it alone to the good pleasure of God's goodness, by which they are distinguished. He is sovereign, and hath mercy on whom he will have mercy, and whom he will, he hardens.

Man hath now a greater dependence on the grace of God than he had before the fall. He depends on the free goodness of God for much more than he did then: then he depended on God's goodness for conferring the reward of perfect obedience: for God was not obliged to promise and bestow that reward: but now we are dependent on the grace of God for much more: we stand in need of grace, not only to bestow glory upon us, but to deliver us from hell and eternal wrath. Under the first covenant we depended on God's goodness to give us the reward of righteousness; and so we do now. And not only so, but we stand in need of God's free and sovereign grace to give us that righteousness; and yet not only so, but we stand in need of his grace to pardon our sin, and release us from the guilt and infinite demerit of it.

And as we are dependent on the goodness of God for more now than under the first covenant, so we are dependent on a much greater, more free and wonderful goodness. We are now more dependent on God's arbitrary and sovereign good pleasure. We were in our first estate dependent on God for holiness: we had our original righteousness from him; but then holiness was not bestowed in such a way of sovereign good pleasure as it is now. Man was created holy, and it became God to create holy all the reasonable creatures he created: it would have been a disparagement to the holiness of God's nature, if he had made an intelligent creature unholy. But now when a man is made holy, it is from mere and arbitrary grace; God may forever deny holiness to the fallen creature if he pleases, without any disparagement to any of his perfections.

And we are not only indeed more dependent on the grace of God, but our dependence is much more conspicuous, because our own insufficiency and helplessness in ourselves is much more apparent in our fallen and undone state, than it was before we were either sinful or miserable. We are more apparently dependent on God for holiness, because we are first sinful, and utterly polluted, and afterwards holy: so the production of the effect is sensible, and its derivation from God more obvious. If man was ever holy and always was so, it would not be so apparent, that he had not holiness necessarily, as an inseparable qualification of human nature. So we are more apparently dependent on free grace for the favor of God, for we are first justly the objects of his displeasure and afterwards are received into favor. We are more apparently dependent on God for happiness, being first miserable, and afterwards happy. It is more apparently free and without merit in us, because we are actually without any kind of excellency to merit, if there could be any such thing as merit in creature excellency. And we are not only without any true excellency, but are full of, and wholly defiled with, that which is infinitely odious. All our good is more apparently from

God, because we are first naked and wholly without any good, and afterwards enriched with all good.

2. We receive all of the power of God. Man's redemption is often spoken of as a work of wonderful power as well as grace. The great power of God appears in bringing a sinner from his low state, from the depths of sin and misery, to such an exalted state of holiness and happiness. Eph. i. 19, "And what is the exceeding greatness of his power to usward who believe, according to the working of his mighty power."

We are dependent on God's power through every step of our redemption. We are dependent on the power of God to convert us, and give faith in Jesus Christ, and the new nature.

It is a work of creation: "If any man be in Christ, he is a new creature," 2 Cor. v. 17. "We are created in Christ Jesus," Eph. ii. 10. The fallen creature cannot attain to true holiness, but by being created again. Eph. iv. 24, "And that ye put on the new man, which after God is created in righteousness and true holiness." It is a raising from the dead. Col. ii. 12, 13, "Wherein ye also are risen with him, through the faith of the operation of God, who hath raised him from the dead." Yea, it is a more glorious work of power than mere creation, or raising a dead body to life, in that the effect attained is greater and more excellent. That holy and happy being, and spiritual life which is reached in the work of conversion, is a far greater and more glorious effect, than mere being and life. And the state from whence the change is made, of such a death in sin, and total corruption of nature, and depth of misery, is far more remote from the state attained, than mere death or nonentity.

It is by God's power also that we are preserved in a state of grace. I Pet. i. 5, "Who are kept by the power of God through faith unto salvation." As grace is at first from God, so it is continually from him, and is maintained

by him, as much as light in the atmosphere is all day long
from the sun, as well as at first dawning, or at sunrising.

Men are dependent on the power of God, for every
exercise of grace, and for carrying on the work of grace
in the heart, for the subduing of sin and corruption, and
increasing holy principles, and enabling to bring forth
fruit in good works, and at last bring grace to its perfection, in making the soul completely amiable in Christ's
glorious likeness, and filling of it with a satisfying joy and
blessedness; and for the raising of the body to life, and
to such a perfect state, that it shall be suitable for a
habitation and organ for a soul so perfected and blessed.
These are the most glorious effects of the power of God,
that are seen in the series of God's acts with respect to
the creatures.

Man was dependent on the power of God in his first
estate, but he is more dependent on his power now; he
needs God's power to do more things for him, and
depends on the more wonderful exercise of his power.
It was an effect of the power of God to make man holy
at the first; but more remarkably so now, because there
is a great deal of opposition and difficulty in the way.
It is a more glorious effect of power to make that holy
that was so depraved, and under the dominion of sin,
than to confer holiness on that which before had nothing
of the contrary. It is a more glorious work of power to
rescue a soul out of the hands of the devil, and from the
powers of darkness, and to bring it into a state of salvation, than to confer holiness where there was no prepos-
session or opposition. Luke xi. 21, 22, "When a strong
man armed keepeth his palace, his goods are in peace;
but when a stronger than he shall come upon him, and
overcome him, he taketh from him all his armor wherein
he trusted, and divideth his spoils." So it is a more
glorious work of power to uphold a soul in a state of
grace and holiness, and to carry it on till it is brought to

glory, when there is so much sin remaining in the heart resisting, and Satan with all his might opposing, than it would have been to have kept man from falling at first, when Satan had nothing in man.

Thus we have shown how the redeemed are dependent on God for all their good, as they have all of him.

SECONDLY. They are also dependent on God for all, as they have all through him. It is God that is the medium of it, as well as the author and fountain of it. All that we have, wisdom, and the pardon of sin, deliverance from hell, acceptance in God's favor, grace and holiness, true comfort and happiness, eternal life and glory, we have from God by a Mediator; and this Mediator is God, which Mediator we have an absolute dependence upon as he through whom we receive all. So that here is another way wherein we have our dependence on God for all good. God not only gives us the Mediator, and accepts his mediation, and of his power and grace bestows the things purchased by the Mediator, but he is the Mediator.

Our blessings are what we have by purchase; and the purchase is made of God, the blessings are purchased of him, and God gives the purchaser; and not only so, but God is the purchaser. Yea, God is both the purchaser and the price; for Christ, who is God, purchased these blessings for us, by offering up himself. Heb. vii. 27, "He offered up himself"; and ix. 26, "He hath appeared to take away sin by the sacrifice of himself." Indeed it was the human nature that was offered; but it was the same person with the divine, and therefore was an infinite price: it was looked upon as if God had been offered in sacrifice.

As we thus have our good through God, we have a dependence on God in a respect that man in his first estate had not. Man was to have eternal life then through his own righteousness; so that he had partly a dependence upon what was in himself; for we have a dependence upon that through which we have our good, as well

as that from which we have it; and though man's righteousness that he then depended on was indeed from God,
yet it was his own, it was inherent in himself; so that his
dependence was not so immediately on God. But now the
righteousness that we are dependent on is not in ourselves, but in God. We are saved through the righteousness of Christ: he *is made unto us righteousness*; and
therefore is prophesied of, Jer. xxiii. 6, under that name,
"the Lord our righteousness." In that the righteousness
we are justified by is the righteousness of Christ, it is the
righteousness of God: 2 Cor. v. 21, "That we might be
made the righteousness of God in him."

Thus in redemption we have not only all things of God,
but by and through him: 1 Cor. viii. 21, "But to us there
is but one God, the Father, of whom are all things, and
we in him; and one Lord Jesus Christ, by whom are all
things, and we by him."

THIRDLY. The redeemed have all their good in God.
We not only have it of him, and through him, but it
consists in him; he is all our good.

The good of the redeemed is either objective or inherent. By their objective good, I mean that extrinsic
object, in the possession and enjoyment of which they are
happy. Their inherent good is that excellency or pleasure
which is in the soul itself. With respect to both of which
the redeemed have all their good in God, or, which is the
same thing, God himself is all their good.

1. The redeemed have all their objective good in God.
God himself is the great good which they are brought to
the possession and enjoyment of by redemption. He is
the highest good, and the sum of all that good which
Christ purchased. God is the inheritance of the saints;
he is the portion of their souls. God is their wealth and
treasure, their food, their life, their dwelling place, their
ornament and diadem, and their everlasting honor and
glory. They have none in heaven but God; he is the great

good which the redeemed are received to at death, and which they are to rise to at the end of the world. The Lord God, he is the light of the heavenly Jerusalem; and is the "river of the water of life," that runs, and "the tree of life that grows, in the midst of the paradise of God." The glorious excellencies and beauty of God will be what will for ever entertain the minds of the saints, and the love of God will be their everlasting feast. The redeemed will indeed enjoy other things; they will enjoy the angels, and will enjoy one another; but that which they shall enjoy in the angels, or each other, or in any thing else whatsoever that will yield them delight and happiness, will be what will be seen of God in them.

2. The redeemed have all their inherent good in God. Inherent good is twofold; it is either excellency or pleasure. These the redeemed not only derive from God, as caused by him, but have them in him. They have spiritual excellency and joy by a kind of participation of God. They are made excellent by a communication of God's excellency: God puts his own beauty, i.e., his beautiful likeness, upon their souls: they are made partakers of the divine nature, or moral image of God, 2 Pet. i. 4. They are holy by being made partakers of God's holiness, Heb. xii. 10. The saints are beautiful and blessed by a communication of God's holiness and joy, as the moon and planets are bright by the sun's light. The saint hath spiritual joy and pleasure by a kind of effusion of God on the soul. In these things the redeemed have communion with God; that is, they partake with him and of him.

The saints have both their spiritual excellency and blessedness by the gift of the Holy Ghost, or Spirit of God, and his dwelling in them. They are not only caused by the Holy Ghost, but are in the Holy Ghost as their principle. The Holy Spirit becoming an inhabitant, is a vital principle in the soul: he, acting in, upon, and with the soul, becomes a fountain of true holiness and joy, as a spring is of water, by the exertion and diffusion of itself. John iv. 14, "But whosoever drinketh of the water that I shall give him, shall never thirst; but the water that I shall give him, shall be in him a well of water springing up into everlasting life." Compared with chap. vii. 38, 39, "He that believeth on me, as the Scripture hath said, out of his belly shall flow rivers of living water; but this spake he of the Spirit, which they that believe on him should receive." The sum of what Christ has purchased for us, is that spring of water spoken of in the former of those places, and those rivers of living water spoken of in the latter. And the sum of the blessings, which the redeemed shall receive in heaven, is that river of water of life that proceeds from the throne of God and the Lamb, Rev. xxii. 1. Which doubtless signifies the same with those rivers of living water, explained, John vii. 38, 39, which is elsewhere called the "river of God's pleasures." Herein consists the fulness of good, which the saints receive by Christ. It is by partaking of the Holy Spirit, that they have communion with Christ in his fulness. God hath given the Spirit, not by measure unto him, and they do receive of his fulness, and grace for grace. This is the sum of the saints' inheritance; and therefore that little of the Holy Ghost which believers have in this world, is said to be the earnest of their inheritance. 2 Cor. i. 22, "Who hath also sealed us, and given us the Spirit in our hearts." And chap. v. 5, "Now he that hath wrought us for the self-same thing, is God, who also hath given unto us the earnest of the Spirit." And Eph. i. 13, 14, "Ye were sealed with that Holy Spirit of promise, which is the earnest of our inheritance, until the redemption of the purchased possession."

The Holy Spirit and good things are spoken of in Scripture as the same; as if the Spirit of God communicated to the soul, comprised all good things: Matt. vii. 11, "How much more shall your heavenly Father give good things to them that ask him?" In Luke it is, chap. xi. 13, "How much more shall your heavenly Father give the Holy Spirit to them that ask him?" This is the sum of the blessings that Christ died to procure, and that are the subject of gospel promises: Gal. iii. 13, 14, "He was made a curse for us, that we might receive the promise of the Spirit through faith." The Spirit of God is the great promise of the Father: Luke xxiv. 49, "Behold, I send the promise of my Father upon you." The Spirit of God therefore is called "the Spirit of promise," Eph. i. 13. This promised thing Christ received, and had given into his hand, as soon as he had finished the work of our redemption, to bestow on all that he had redeemed: Acts ii. 33, "Therefore, being by the right hand of God exalted, and having received of the Father the promise of the Holy Ghost, he hath shed forth this, which ye both see and hear." So that all the holiness and happiness of the redeemed is in God. It is in the communications, indwelling, and acting of the Spirit of God. Holiness and happiness are in the fruit, here and hereafter, because God dwells in them, and they in God.

Thus it is God that has given us the Redeemer, and it is of him that our good is purchased: so it is God that is the Redeemer, and the price; and it is God also that is the good purchased. So that all that we have is of God, and through him, and in him: Rom. xi. 36, "For of him, and through him, and to him, or in him, are all things." The same in the Greek that is here rendered *to him*, is rendered *in him*, 1 Cor. xii. 6.

II. God is glorified in the work of redemption by this means, viz., by there being so great and universal a dependence of the redeemed on him.

1. Man hath so much the greater occasion and obligation to take notice and acknowledge God's perfections and all-sufficiency. The greater the creature's dependence is on God's perfections, and the greater concern he has

with them, so much the greater occasion has he to take notice of them. So much the greater concern any one has with, and dependence upon, the power and grace of God, so much the greater occasion has he to take notice of that power and grace. So much the greater and more immediate dependence there is on the divine holiness, so much the greater occasion to take notice of, and acknowledge that. So much the greater and more absolute dependence we have on the divine perfections, as belonging to the several persons of the Trinity, so much the greater occasion have we to observe and own the divine glory of each of them. That which we are most concerned with, is surely most in the way of our observation and notice; and this kind of concern with any thing, viz., dependence, does especially tend to command and oblige the attention and observation. Those things that we are not much dependent upon, it is easy to neglect; but we can scarce do any other than mind that which we have a great dependence on. By reason of our so great dependence on God, and his perfections, and in so many respects, he and his glory are the more directly set in our view, which way soever we turn our eyes.

We have the greater occasion to take notice of God's all-sufficiency, when all our sufficiency is thus every way of him. We have the more occasion to contemplate him as an infinite good, and as the fountain of all good. Such a dependence on God, demonstrates God's all-sufficiency. So much the dependence of the creature is on God, so much the greater does the creature's emptiness in himself appear to be; and so much the greater the creature's emptiness, so much the greater must the fulness of the Being be who supplies him. Our having all of God shows the fulness of his power and grace: our having all through him shows the fulness of his merit and worthiness; and our having all in him demonstrates his fulness of beauty, love, and happiness.

And the redeemed, by reason of the greatness of their dependence on God, have not only so much the greater occasion, but obligation to contemplate and acknowledge the glory and fulness of God. How unreasonable and ungrateful should we be if we did not acknowledge that sufficiency and glory that we do absolutely, immediately, and universally depend upon!

2. Hereby is demonstrated how great God's glory is considered comparatively, or as compared with the creature's. By the creature's being thus wholly and universally dependent on God, it appears that the creature is nothing, and that God is all. Hereby it appears that God is infinitely above us; that God's strength, and wisdom, and holiness, are infinitely greater than ours. However great and glorious the creature apprehends God to be, yet if he be not sensible of the difference between God and him, so as to see that God's glory is great, compared with his own, he will not be disposed to give God the glory due to his name. If the creature, in any respect, sets himself upon a level with God, or exalts himself to any competition with him, however he may apprehend that great honor and profound respect may belong to God from those that are more inferior, and at a greater distance, he will not be so sensible of its being due from him. So much the more men exalt themselves, so much the less will they surely be disposed to exalt God. It is certainly a thing that God aims at in the disposition of things in the affair of redemption (if we allow the Scriptures to be a revelation of God's mind), that God should appear all, and man nothing. It is God's declared design that others should not "glory in his presence"; which implies that it is his design to advance his own comparative glory. So much the more man "glories in God's presence," so much the less glory is ascribed to God.

3. By its being thus ordered, that the creature should have so absolute and universal a dependence on God,

provision is made that God should have our whole souls, and should be the object of our undivided respect. If we had our dependence partly on God, and partly on something else, man's respect would be divided to those different things on which he had dependence. Thus it would be if we depended on God only for a part of our good, and on ourselves, or some other being for another part: or if we had our good only from God, and through another that was not God, and in something else distinct from both, our hearts would be divided between the good itself, and him from whom, and him through whom we received it. But now there is no occasion for this, God being not only he from or of whom we have all good, but also through whom and one that is that good itself, that we have from him and through him. So that whatsoever there is to attract our respect, the tendency is still directly towards God, all units in him as the centre.

Use

1. We may here observe the marvellous wisdom of God, in the work of redemption. God hath made man's emptiness and misery, his low, lost and ruined state into which he sunk by the fall, an occasion of the greater advancement of his own glory, as in other ways, so particularly in this, that there is now a much more universal and apparent dependence of man on God. Though God be pleased to lift man out of that dismal abyss of sin and woe into which he was fallen, and exceedingly to exalt him in excellency and honor, and to a high pitch of glory and blessedness, yet the creature hath nothing in any respect to glory of; all the glory evidently belongs to God, all is in a mere, and most absolute and divine dependence on the Father, Son, and Holy Ghost.

And each person of the Trinity is equally glorified in this work: there is an absolute dependence of the creature on every one for all: all is of the Father, all through the Son, and all in the Holy Ghost. Thus God appears in the work of redemption as all in all. It is fit that he that is, and there is none else, should be the Alpha and Omega, the first and the last, the all, and the only, in this work.

2. Hence those doctrines and schemes of divinity that are in any respect opposite to such an absolute and universal dependence on God, do derogate from God's glory, and thwart the design of the contrivance for our redemption. Those schemes that put the creature in God's stead, in any of the forementioned respects, that exalt man into the place of either Father, Son, or Holy Ghost, in any thing pertaining to our redemption; that, however they may allow of a dependence of the redeemed on God, yet deny a dependence that is so absolute and universal; that own an entire dependence on God for some things, but not for others; that own that we depend on God for the gift and acceptance of a Redeemer, but deny so absolute a dependence on Him for the obtaining of an interest in the Redeemer; that own an absolute dependence on the Father for giving his Son, and on the Son for working out redemption, but not so entire a dependence on the Holy Ghost for conversion, and a being in Christ, and so coming to a title to his benefits; that own a dependence on God for means of grace, but not absolutely for the benefit and success of those means; that own a partial dependence on the power of God, for the obtaining and exercising holiness, but not a mere dependence on the arbitrary and sovereign grace of God that own a dependence on the free grace of God for a reception into his favor, so far that it is without any proper merit, but not as it is without being attracted, or moved with any excellency; that own a partial dependence on Christ, as he through whom we have life, as having purchased new terms of life, but still hold that the righteousness through which we have life is inherent in ourselves, as it was under the

first covenant; and whatever other way any scheme is inconsistent with our entire dependence on God for all, and in each of those ways, of having all of him, through him, and in him, it is repugnant to the design and tenor of the gospel, and robs it of that which God accounts its lustre and glory.

3. Hence we may learn a reason why faith is that by which we come to have an interest in this redemption; for there is included in the nature of faith, a sensibleness and acknowledgment of this absolute dependence on God in this affair. It is very fit that it should be required of all, in order to their having the benefit of this redemption, that they should be sensible of, and acknowledge their dependence on God for it. It is by this means that God hath contrived to glorify himself in redemption; and it is fit that God should at least have this glory of those that are the subjects of this redemption, and have the benefit of it.

Faith is a sensibleness of what is real in the work of redemption; and as we do really wholly depend on God, so the soul that believes doth entirely depend on God for all salvation, in its own sense and act. Faith abases men, and exalts God, it gives all the glory of redemption to God alone. It is necessary in order to saving faith, that man should be emptied of himself, that he should be sensible that he is "wretched, and miserable, and poor, and blind, and naked." Humility is a great ingredient of true faith: he that truly receives redemption, receives it as a little child. Mark x. 15, "Whosoever shall not receive the kingdom of heaven as a little child, he shall not enter therein." It is the delight of a believing soul to abase itself and exalt God alone: that is the language of it, Psalm cxv. 1, "Not unto us, O Lord, not unto us, but to thy name give glory."

4. Let us be exhorted to exalt God alone, and ascribe to him all the glory of redemption. Let us endeavor to

obtain, and increase in a sensibleness of our great dependence on God, to have our eye to him alone, to mortify a self-dependent, and self-righteous disposition. Man is naturally exceeding prone to be exalting himself and depending on his own power or goodness, as though he were he from whom he must expect happiness, and to have respect to enjoyments alien from God and his Spirit, as those in which happiness is to be found.

And this doctrine should teach us to exalt God alone, as by trust and reliance, so by praise. *Let him that glorieth, glory in the Lord.* Hath any man hope that he is converted, and sanctified, and that his mind is endowed with true excellency and spiritual beauty, and his sins forgiven, and he received into God's favor, and exalted to the honor and blessedness of being his child, and an heir of eternal life; let him give God all the glory; who alone makes him to differ from the worst of men in this world, or the miserablest of the damned in hell. Hath any man much comfort and strong hope of eternal life, let not his hope lift him up, but dispose him the more to abase himself, and reflect on his own exceeding unworthiness of such a favor, and to exalt God alone. Is any man eminent in holiness, and abundant in good works, let him take nothing of the glory of it to himself, but ascribe it to him whose "workmanship we are created in Christ Jesus unto good works."

A DIVINE AND
SUPERNATURAL LIGHT

MATTHEW xvi. 17.—And Jesus answered and said
unto him, Blessed art thou, Simon Barjona: for flesh
and blood hath not revealed it unto thee, but my Father
which is in heaven.

Christ says these words to Peter upon occasion of his
professing his faith in him as the Son of God. Our Lord
was inquiring of his disciples, who men said he was;
not that he needed to be informed, but only to introduce
and give occasion to what follows. They answer, that
some said he was John the Baptist, and some Elias, and
others Jeremias, or one of the Prophets. When they had
thus given an account who others said he was, Christ
asks them, who they said he was? Simon Peter, whom we
find always zealous and forward, was the first to answer:
he readily replied to the question, *Thou art Christ, the
Son of the living God.*

Upon this occasion, Christ says as he does TO him,
and OF him in the text: in which we may observe,

1. That Peter is pronounced blessed on this account.
BLESSED ART THOU.—"Thou art a happy man, that
thou art not ignorant of this, that I am CHRIST, THE
SON OF THE LIVING GOD. Thou art distinguishingly
happy. Others are blinded and have dark and deluded
apprehensions, as you have now given an account, some
thinking that I am Elias, and some that I am Jeremias,
and some one thing, and some another; but none of them
thinking right, all of them misled. Happy art thou, that
art so distinguished as to know the truth in this matter."

2. The evidence of this his happiness declared; viz., that God, and he ONLY, had REVEALED IT to him. This is an evidence of his being BLESSED.

FIRST. As it shows how peculiarly favored he was of God above others; q. d., "How highly favored art thou, that others that are wise and great men, the Scribes, Pharisees, and Rulers, and the nation in general, are left in darkness, to follow their own misguided apprehensions; and that thou shouldst be singled out, as it were, by name, that my Heavenly Father should thus set his love, on THEE, SIMON BARJONA. This argues thee blessed, that thou shouldst thus be the object of God's distinguishing love."

SECONDLY. It evidences his blessedness also, as it intimates that this knowledge is above any that FLESH and BLOOD can REVEAL. "This is such knowledge as my FATHER WHICH IS IN HEAVEN only can give: it is too high and excellent to be communicated by such means as other knowledge is. Thou art BLESSED, that thou knowest that which God alone can teach thee."

The original of this knowledge is here declared, both negatively and positively. POSITIVELY, as God is here declared the author of it. NEGATIVELY, as it is declared, that flesh and blood had not revealed it. God is the author of all knowledge and understanding whatsoever. He is the author of the knowledge that is obtained by human learning: he is the author of all moral prudence, and of the knowledge and skill that men have in their secular business. Thus it is said of all in Israel that were wise-hearted, and skilful in embroidering, that God had filled them with the spirit of wisdom, Exod. xxviii. 3.

God is the author of such knowledge; but yet not so but that FLESH and BLOOD reveals it. Mortal men are capable of imparting the knowledge of human arts and sciences, and skill in temporal affairs. God is the author of such knowledge by those means: FLESH and BLOOD is made use of by God as the mediate or second cause of it; he conveys it by the power and influence of natural means. But this spiritual knowledge, spoken of in the text, is what God is the author of, and none else: he reveals it, and FLESH and BLOOD reveals it not. He imparts this knowledge immediately, not making use of any intermediate natural causes, as he does in other knowledge.

What had passed in the preceding discourse naturally occasioned Christ to observe this; because the disciples had been telling how others did not know him, but were generally mistaken about him, and divided and confounded in their opinions of him: but Peter had declared his assured faith, that he was the Son of God. Now it was natural to observe, how it was not FLESH and BLOOD that had revealed it to him, but God: for if this knowledge were dependent on natural causes or means, how came it to pass that they, a company of poor fishermen, illiterate men, and persons of low education, attained to the knowledge of the truth; while the Scribes and Pharisees, men of vastly higher advantages, and greater knowledge and sagacity in other matters, remained in ignorance? This could be owing only to the gracious distinguishing influence and revelation of the Spirit of God. Hence, what I would make the subject of my present discourse from these words, is this

Doctrine

That there is such a thing as a Spiritual and Divine Light, immediately imparted to the soul by God, of a different nature from any that is obtained by natural means.

In what I say on this subject, at this time, I would,

I. Show what this divine light is.

II. How it is given immediately by God, and not obtained by natural means.

III. Show the truth of the doctrine.

And then conclude with a brief improvement.

I. I would show what this spiritual and divine light is. And in order to it, would show,

FIRST, In a few things what it is not. And here,

1. Those convictions that natural men may have of their sin and misery, is not this spiritual and divine light. Men in a natural condition may have convictions of the guilt that lies upon them, and of the anger of God, and their danger of divine vengeance. Such convictions are from light or sensibleness of truth. That some sinners have a greater conviction of their guilt and misery than others, is because some have more light, or more of an apprehension of truth than others. And this light and conviction may be from the Spirit of God; the Spirit convinces men of sin: but yet nature is much more concerned in it than in the communication of that spiritual and divine light that is spoken of in the doctrine; it is from the Spirit of God only as assisting natural principles, and not as infusing any new principles. Common grace differs from special, in that it influences only by assisting of nature; and not by imparting grace, or bestowing any thing above nature. The light that is obtained is wholly natural, or of no superior kind to what mere nature attains to, though more of that kind be obtained than would be obtained if men were left wholly to themselves: or, in other words, common grace only assists the faculties of the soul to do that more fully which they do by nature, as natural conscience or reason will, by mere nature, make a man sensible of guilt, and will accuse and condemn him when he has done amiss. Conscience is a principle natural to men; and the work that it doth naturally, or of itself, is to give an apprehension of right and wrong, and to suggest to the mind the relation that there is between right and wrong, and a retribution. The Spirit of God, in those convictions which unregenerate men sometimes have, assists conscience to do this work in a

further degree than it would do if they were left to themselves: he helps it against those things that tend to stupify it, and obstruct its exercise. But in the renewing and sanctifying work of the Holy Ghost, those things are wrought in the soul that are above nature, and of which there is nothing of the like kind in the soul by nature; and they are caused to exist in the soul habitually, and according to such a stated constitution or law that lays such a foundation for exercises in a continued course, as is called a principle of nature. Not only are remaining principles assisted to do their work more freely and fully, but those principles are restored that were utterly destroyed by the fall; and the mind thenceforward habitually exerts those acts that the dominion of sin had made it as wholly destitute of, as a dead body is of vital acts.

The Spirit of God acts in a very different manner in the one case, from what he doth in the other. He may indeed act upon the mind of a natural man, but he acts in the mind of a saint as an indwelling vital principle. He acts upon the mind of an unregenerate person as an extrinsic, occasional agent; for in acting upon them, he doth not unite himself to them; for notwithstanding all his influences that they may be the subjects of, they are still sensual, having not the Spirit, Jude 19. But he unites himself with the mind of a saint, takes him for his temple, actuates and influences him as a new supernatural principle of life and action. There is this difference, that the Spirit of God, in acting in the soul of a godly man, exerts and communicates himself there in his own proper nature. Holiness is the proper nature of the Spirit of God. The Holy Spirit operates in the minds of the godly, by uniting himself to them, and living in them, and exerting his own nature in the exercise of their faculties. The Spirit of God may act upon a creature, and yet not in acting communicate himself. The Spirit of God may act upon inanimate creatures; as, the *Spirit moved upon the face of the waters,* in the beginning of the creation; so the Spirit of God may act upon the minds of men many ways, and communicate himself no more than when he acts upon an inanimate creature. For instance, he may excite thoughts in them, may assist their natural reason and understanding, or may assist other natural principles, and this without any union with the soul, but may act, as it were, as upon an external object. But as he acts in his holy influences and spiritual operations, he acts in a way of peculiar communication of himself; so that the subject is thence denominated spiritual.

2. This spiritual and divine light does not consist in any impression made upon the imagination. It is no impression upon the mind, as though one saw any thing with the bodily eyes: it is no imagination or idea of an outward light or glory, or any beauty of form or countenance, or a visible lustre or brightness of any object. The imagination may be strongly impressed with such things; but this is not spiritual light. Indeed when the mind has a lively discovery of spiritual things, and is greatly affected by the power of divine light, it may, and probably very commonly doth, much affect the imagination; so that impressions of an outward beauty or brightness may accompany those spiritual discoveries. But spiritual light is not that impression upon the imagination, but an exceeding different thing from it. Natural men may have lively impressions on their imaginations; and we cannot determine but the devil, who transforms himself into an angel of light, may cause imaginations of an outward beauty, or visible glory, and of sounds and speeches, and other such things; but these are things of a vastly inferior nature to spiritual light.

3. This spiritual light is not the suggesting of any new truths or propositions not contained in the word of God. This suggesting of new truths or doctrines to the mind, independent of any antecedent revelation of those propositions, either in word or writing, is inspiration; such

as the prophets and apostles had, and such as some enthusiasts pretend to. But this spiritual light that I am speaking of, is quite a different thing from inspiration: it reveals no new doctrine, it suggests no new proposition to the mind, it teaches no new thing of God, or Christ, or another world, not taught in the Bible, but only gives a due apprehension of those things that are taught in the word of God.

4. It is not every affecting view that men have of the things of religion that is this spiritual and divine light. Men by mere principles of nature are capable of being affected with things that have a special relation to religion as well as other things. A person by mere nature, for instance, may be liable to be affected with the story of Jesus Christ, and the sufferings he underwent, as well as by any other tragical story: he may be the more affected with it from the interest he conceives mankind to have in it: yea, he may be affected with it without believing it; as well as a man may be affected with what he reads in a romance, or sees acted in a stage play. He may be affected with a lively and eloquent description of many pleasant things that attend the state of the blessed in heaven, as well as his imagination be entertained by a romantic description of the pleasantness of fairy land, or the like. And that common belief of the truth of the things of religion, that persons may have from education or otherwise, may help forward their affection. We read in Scripture of many that were greatly affected with things of a religious nature, who yet are there represented as wholly graceless, and many of them very ill men. A person therefore may have affecting views of the things of religion, and yet be very destitute of spiritual light. Flesh and blood may be the author of this: one man may give another an affecting view of divine things with but common assistance: but God alone can give a spiritual discovery of them.

But I proceed to show,

SECONDLY, Positively what this spiritual and divine light is.

And it may be thus described: a true sense of the divine excellency of the things revealed in the word of God, and a conviction of the truth and reality of them thence arising.

This spiritual light primarily consists in the former of these, viz., a real sense and apprehension of the divine excellency of things revealed in the word of God. A spiritual and saving conviction of the truth and reality of these things, arises from such a sight of their divine excellency and glory; so that this conviction of their truth is an effect and natural consequence of this sight of their divine glory. There is therefore in this spiritual light,

1. A true sense of the divine and superlative excellency of the things of religion; a real sense of the excellency of God and Jesus Christ, and of the work of redemption, and the ways and works of God revealed in the gospel. There is a divine and superlative glory in these things; an excellency that is of a vastly higher kind, and more sublime nature than in other things; a glory greatly distinguishing them from all that is earthly and temporal. He that is spiritually enlightened truly apprehends and sees it, or has a sense of it. He does not merely rationally believe that God is glorious, but he has a sense of the gloriousness of God in his heart. There is not only a rational belief that God is holy, and that holiness is a good thing, but there is a sense of the liveliness of God's holiness. There is not only a speculatively judging that God is gracious, but a sense how amiable God is upon that account, or a sense of the beauty of this divine attribute.

There is a twofold understanding or knowledge of good that God has made the mind of man capable of. The first, that which is merely speculative and notional; as when a person only speculatively judges that any thing is, which, by the agreement of mankind, is called good or excellent, viz., that which is most to general advantage, and between which and a reward there is a suitableness, and the like. And the other is, that which consists in the sense of the heart: as when there is a sense of the beauty, amiableness, or sweetness of a thing; so that the heart is sensible of pleasure and delight in the presence of the idea of it. In the former is exercised merely the speculative faculty, or the understanding, strictly so called, or as spoken of in distinction from the will or disposition of the soul. In the latter, the will, or inclination, or heart, is mainly concerned.

Thus there is a difference between having an opinion, that God is holy and gracious, and having a sense of the loveliness and beauty of that holiness and grace. There is a difference between having a rational judgment that honey is sweet, and having a sense of its sweetness. A man may have the former, that knows not how honey tastes; but a man cannot have the latter unless he has an idea of the taste of honey in his mind. So there is a difference between believing that a person is beautiful, and having a sense of his beauty. The former may be obtained by hearsay, but the latter only by seeing the countenance. There is a wide difference between mere speculative rational judging any thing to be excellent, and having a sense of its sweetness and beauty. The former rests only in the head, speculation only is concerned in it; but the heart is concerned in the latter. When the heart is sensible of the beauty and amiableness of a thing, it necessarily feels pleasure in the apprehension. It is implied in a person's being heartily sensible of the loveliness of a thing, that the idea of it is sweet and pleasant to his soul; which is a far different thing from having a rational opinion that it is excellent.

2. There arises from this sense of divine excellency of

things contained in the word of God, a conviction of the truth and reality of them; and that either directly or indirectly.

First, indirectly, and that two ways.

1. As the prejudices that are in the heart, against the truth of divine things, are hereby removed; so that the mind becomes susceptive of the due force of rational arguments for their truth. The mind of man is naturally full of prejudices against the truth of divine things: it is full of enmity against the doctrines of the gospel; which is a disadvantage to those arguments that prove their truth, and causes them to lose their force upon the mind. But when a person has discovered to him the divine excellency of Christian doctrines, this destroys the enmity, removes those prejudices, and sanctifies the reason, and causes it to lie open to the force of arguments for their truth.

Hence was the different effect that Christ's miracles had to convince the disciples from what they had to convince the Scribes and Pharisees. Not that they had a stronger reason, or had their reason more improved; but their reason was sanctified, and those blinding prejudices, that the Scribes and Pharisees were under, were removed by the sense they had of the excellency of Christ and his doctrine.

2. It not only removes the hindrances of reason, but positively helps reason. It makes even the speculative notions the more lively. It engages the attention of the mind, with the more fixedness and intenseness to that kind of objects; which causes it to have a clearer view of them, and enables it more clearly to see their mutual relations, and occasions it to take more notice of them. The ideas themselves that otherwise are dim and obscure, are by this means impressed with the greater strength, and have a light cast upon them; so that the mind can better judge of them. As he that beholds the objects on

the face of the earth, when the light of the sun is cast upon them, is under greater advantage to discern them in their true forms and mutual relations, than he that sees them in a dim starlight or twilight.

The mind having a sensibleness of the excellency of divine objects, dwells upon them with delight; and the powers of the soul are more awakened and enlivened to employ themselves in the contemplation of them, and exert themselves more fully and much more to the purpose. The beauty and sweetness of the objects draws on the faculties, and draws forth their exercises: so that reason itself is under far greater advantages for its proper and free exercises, and to attain its proper end, free of darkness and delusion. But,

SECONDLY. A true sense of the divine excellency of the things of God's word doth more directly and immediately convince of the truth of them; and that because the excellency of these things is so superlative. There is a beauty in them that is so divine and godlike, that is greatly and evidently distinguishing of them from things merely human, or that men are the inventors and authors of; a glory that is so high and great, that when clearly seen, commands assent to their divinity and reality. When there is an actual and lively discovery of this beauty and excellency, it will not allow of any such thought as that it is a human work, or the fruit of men's invention. This evidence that they that are spiritually enlightened have of the truth of the things of religion, is a kind of intuitive and immediate evidence. They believe the doctrines of God's word to be divine, because they see divinity in them; i.e., they see a divine, and transcendent, and most evidently distinguishing glory in them; such a glory as, if clearly seen, does not leave room to doubt of their being of God, and not of men.

Such a conviction of the truth of religion as this, arising, these ways, from a sense of the divine excellency of them, is that true spiritual conviction that there is in saving faith. And this original of it, is that by which it is most essentially distinguished from that common assent, which unregenerate men are capable of.

II. I proceed now to the second thing proposed, viz., to show how this light is immediately given by God, and not obtained by natural means. And here,

1. It is not intended that the natural faculties are not made use of in it. The natural faculties are the subject of this light: and they are the subject in such a manner, that they are not merely passive, but active in it; the acts and exercises of man's understanding are concerned and made use of in it. God, in letting in this light into the soul, deals with man according to his nature, or as a rational creature; and makes use of his human faculties. But yet this light is not the less immediately from God for that; though the faculties are made use of, it is as the subject and not as the cause; and that acting of the faculties in it, is not the cause, but is either implied in the thing itself (in the light that is imparted) or is the consequence of it. As the use that we make of our eyes in beholding various objects, when the sun arises, is not the cause of the light that discovers those objects to us.

2. It is not intended that outward means have no concern in this affair. As I have observed already, it is not in this affair, as it is in inspiration, where new truths are suggested: for here is by this light only given a due apprehension of the same truths that are revealed in the word of God; and therefore it is not given without the word. The gospel is made use of in this affair: this light is the light of the glorious gospel of Christ, 2 Cor. iv. 4. The gospel is as a glass, by which this light is conveyed to us, 1 Cor. xiii. 12. Now we see through a glass.—But,

3. When it is said that this light is given immediately by God, and not obtained by natural means, hereby is intended, that it is given by God without making use of

any means that operate by their own power, or a natural force. God makes use of means; but it is not as mediate causes to produce this effect. There are not truly any second causes of it; but it is produced by God immediately. The word of God is no proper cause of this effect: it does not operate by any natural force in it. The word of God is only made use of to convey to the mind the subject matter of this saving instruction: and this indeed it doth convey to us by natural force or influence. It conveys to our minds these and those doctrines; it is the cause of the notion of them in our heads, but not of the sense of the divine excellency of them in our hearts. Indeed a person cannot have spiritual light without the word. But that does not argue, that the word properly causes that light. The mind cannot see the excellency of any doctrine, unless that doctrine be first in the mind; but the seeing of the excellency of the doctrine may be immediately from the Spirit of God; though the conveying of the doctrine or proposition itself may be by the word. So that the notions that are the subject matter of this light, are conveyed to the mind by the word of God; but that due sense of the heart, wherein this light formally consists, is immediately by the Spirit of God. As for instance, that notion that there is a Christ, and that Christ is holy and gracious, is conveyed to the mind by the word of God: but the sense of the excellency of Christ by reason of that holiness and grace, is nevertheless immediately the work of the Holy Spirit.

I come now,

III. To show the truth of the doctrine; that is, to show that there is such a thing as that spiritual light that has been described, thus immediately let into the mind by God. And here I would show briefly, that this doctrine is both *scriptural* and *rational*.

FIRST. It is scriptural. My text is not only full to the purpose, but it is a doctrine that the Scripture abounds in. We are there abundantly taught, that the saints differ from the ungodly in this, that they have the knowledge of God, and a sight of God, and of Jesus Christ. I shall mention but few texts of many. 1 John iii. 6, "Whosoever sinneth, has not seen him, nor known him." 3 John 11, "He that doth good, is of God: but he that doth evil, hath not seen God." John xiv. 19, "The world seeth me no more; but ye see me." John xvii. 3, "And this is eternal life, that they might know thee, the only true God, and Jesus Christ whom thou hast sent." This knowledge, or sight of God and Christ, cannot be a mere speculative knowledge; because it is spoken of as a seeing and knowing, wherein they differ from the ungodly. And by these Scriptures it must not only be a different knowledge in degree and circumstances, and different in its effects; but it must be entirely different in nature and kind.

And this light and knowledge is always spoken of as immediately given of God, Matt. xi. 25, 26, 27: "At that time Jesus answered and said, I thank thee O Father, Lord of heaven and earth, because thou hast hid these things from the wise and prudent, and hast revealed them unto babes. Even so, Father, for so it seemed good in thy sight. All things are delivered unto me of my Father: and no man knoweth the Son, but the Father: neither knoweth any man the Father, save the Son, and he to whomsoever the Son will reveal him." Here this effect is ascribed alone to the arbitrary operation, and gift of God, bestowing this knowledge on whom he will, and distinguishing those with it, that have the least natural advantage or means for knowledge, even babes, when it is denied to the wise and prudent. And the imparting of the knowledge of God is here appropriated to the Son of God, as his sole prerogative. And again, 2 Cor. iv. 6, "For God, who commanded the light to shine out of darkness, hath shined in our hearts, to give the light of the knowledge of the glory of God, in the face of Jesus

Christ." This plainly shows, that there is such a thing as a discovery of the divine superlative glory and excellency of God and Christ, and that peculiar to the saints: and also, that it is as immediately from God, as light from the sun: and that it is the immediate effect of his power and will; for it is compared to God's creating the light by his powerful word in the beginning of the creation; and is said to be by the Spirit of the Lord, in the 18th verse of the preceding chapter. God is spoken of as giving the knowledge of Christ in conversion, as of what before was hidden and unseen in that. Gal. i. 15, 16, "But when it pleased God, who separated me from my mother's womb, and called me by his grace, to reveal his Son in me." The Scripture also speaks plainly of such a knowledge of the word of God, as has been described, as the immediate gift of God, Psal. cxix. 18: "Open thou mine eyes, that I may behold wondrous things out of thy law." What could the Psalmist mean when he begged of God to open his eyes? Was he ever blind? Might he not have resort to the law and see every word and sentence in it when he pleased? And what could he mean by those wondrous things? Was it the wonderful stories of the creation, and deluge, and Israel's passing through the Red Sea, and the like? Were not his eyes open to read these strange things when he would? Doubtless by wondrous things in God's law, he had respect to those distinguishing and wonderful excellencies, and marvellous manifestations of the divine perfections, and glory, that there was in the commands and doctrines of the word, and those works and counsels of God that were there revealed. So the Scripture speaks of a knowledge of God's dispensation, and covenant of mercy, and way of grace towards his people, as peculiar to the saints, and given only by God, Psal. xxv. 14: "The secret of the Lord is with them that fear him; and he will show them his covenant."

And that a true and saving belief of the truth of

religion is that which arises from such a discovery, is also what the Scripture teaches. As John vi. 40, "And this is the will of him that sent me, that very one which seeth the Son, and believeth on him, may have everlasting life"; where it is plain that a true faith is what arises from a spiritual sight of Christ. And John xvii. 6, 7, 8, "I have manifested thy name unto the men which thou gavest me out of the world. Now they have known that all things whatsoever thou hast given me, are of thee. For I have given unto them the words which thou gavest me; and they have received them, and have known surely that I came out from thee, and they have believed that thou didst send me"; where Christ's manifesting God's name to the disciples, or giving them the knowledge of God, was that whereby they knew that Christ's doctrine was of God, and that Christ himself was of him, proceeded from him, and was sent by him. Again, John xii. 44, 45, 46, "Jesus cried and said, He that believeth on me, believeth not on me, but on him that sent me. And he that seeth me, seeth him that sent me. I am come a light into the world, that whosoever believeth on me, should not abide in darkness." Their believing in Christ, and spiritually seeing him, are spoken of as running parallel.

Christ condemns the Jews, that they did not know that he was the Messiah, and that his doctrine was true, from an inward distinguishing taste and relish of what was divine, in Luke xii. 56, 57. He having there blamed the Jews, that though they could discern the face of the sky and of the earth, and signs of the weather, that yet they could not discern those times; or as it is expressed in Matthew, the signs of those times; he adds, yea, and why even of your own selves, judge ye not what is right? i.e., without extrinsic signs. Why have ye not that sense of true excellency, whereby ye may distinguish that which is holy and divine? Why have ye not that savor of the things of God, by which you may see the distinguishing glory, and evident divinity of me and my doctrine?

The Apostle Peter mentions it as what gave them (the apostles) good and well grounded assurance of the truth of the gospel, that they had seen the divine glory of Christ. 2 Pet. i. 16, "For we have not followed cunningly devised fables when we made known unto you the power and coming of our Lord Jesus Christ, but were eyewitnesses of his majesty." The apostle has respect to that visible glory of Christ which they saw in his transfiguration: that glory was so divine, having such an ineffable appearance and semblance of divine holiness, majesty and grace, that it evidently denoted him to be a divine person. But if a sight of Christ's outward glory might give a rational assurance of his divinity, why may not an apprehension of his spiritual glory do so too? Doubtless Christ's spiritual glory is in itself as distinguishing, and as plainly showing his divinity, as his outward glory, and a great deal more: for his spiritual glory is that wherein his divinity consists; and the outward glory of his transfiguration showed him to be divine, only as it was a remarkable image or representation of that spiritual glory. Doubtless, therefore, he that has had a clear sight of the spiritual glory of Christ, may say, I have not followed cunningly devised fables, but have been an eyewitness of his majesty, upon as good grounds as the apostle, when he had respect to the outward glory of Christ that he had seen.

But this brings me to what was proposed next, viz., to show that,

SECONDLY, This doctrine is rational.

1. It is rational to suppose, that there is really such an excellency in divine things, that is so transcendent and exceedingly different from what is in other things, that, if it were seen, would most evidently distinguish them. We cannot rationally doubt but that things that are divine, that appertain to the Supreme Being, are vastly different from things that are human; that there is that godlike, high and glorious excellency in them, that does most

remarkably difference them from the things that are of men; insomuch that if the difference were but seen, it would have a convincing, satisfying influence upon any one, that they are what they are, viz., divine. What reason can be offered against it? Unless we would argue, that God is not remarkably distinguished in glory from men.

If Christ should now appear to any one as he did on the mount at his transfiguration; or if he should appear to the world in the glory that he now appears in, as he will do at the day of judgment; without doubt, the glory and majesty that he would appear in, would be such as would satisfy every one, that he was a divine person, and that religion was true: and it would be a most reasonable, and well grounded conviction too. And why may there not be that stamp of divinity, or divine glory on the word of God, on the scheme and doctrine of the gospel, that may be in like manner distinguishing and as rationally convincing, provided it be but seen? It is rational to suppose, that when God speaks to the world, there should be something in his word or speech vastly different from man's word. Supposing that God never had spoken to the world, but we had noticed that he was about to do it; that he was about to reveal himself from heaven, and speak to us immediately himself, in divine speeches or discourses, as it were from his own mouth, or that he should give us a book of his own inditing; after what manner should we expect that he would speak? Would it not be rational to suppose, that his speech would be exceeding different from man's speech, that he should speak like a God; that is, that there should be such an excellency and sublimity in his speech or word, such a stamp of wisdom, holiness, majesty and other divine perfections, that the word of man, yea of the wisest of men, should appear mean and base in comparison of it? Doubtless it would be thought rational to expect this, and unreasonable to think otherwise. When a wise man speaks in the exercise of his wisdom, there is something in every thing he says, that is very distinguishable from the talk of a little child. So, without doubt, and much more, is the speech of God (if there be any such thing as the speech of God) to be distinguished from that of the wisest of men; agreeably to Jer. xxiii. 28, 29. God having there been reproving the false prophets that prophesied in his name, and pretended that what they spake was his word, when indeed it was their own word, says, "The prophet that hath a dream, let him tell a dream; and he that hath my word, let him speak my word faithfully; what is the chaff to the wheat? saith the Lord. Is not my word like as a fire? saith the Lord; and like a hammer that breaketh the rock in pieces?"

2. If there be such a distinguishing excellency in divine things; it is rational to suppose that there may be such a thing as seeing it. What should hinder but that it may be seen? It is no argument, that there is no such thing as such a distinguishing excellency, or that, if there be, that it cannot be seen, that some do not see it, though they may be discerning men in temporal matters. It is not rational to suppose, if there be any such excellency in divine things, that wicked men should see it. It is not rational to suppose, that those whose minds are full of spiritual pollution, and under the power of filthy lusts, should have any relish or sense of divine beauty or excellency; or that their minds should be susceptive of that light that is in its own nature so pure and heavenly. It need not seem at all strange, that sin should so blind the mind, seeing that men's particular natural tempers and dispositions will so much blind them in secular matters; as when men's natural temper is melancholy, jealous, fearful, proud, or the like.

3. It is rational to suppose, that this knowledge should be given immediately by God, and not be obtained by natural means. Upon what account should it seem un-

reasonable, that there should be any immediate communication between God and the creature? It is strange that men should make any matter of difficulty of it. Why should not he that made all things, still have something immediately to do with the things that he has made? Where lies the great difficulty, if we own the being of a God, and that he created all things out of nothing, of allowing some immediate influence of God on the creation still? And if it be reasonable to suppose it with respect to any part of the creation, it is especially so with respect to reasonable, intelligent creatures; who are next to God in the gradation of the different orders of beings, and whose business is most immediately with God; who were made on purpose for those exercises that do respect God and wherein they have nextly to do with God: for reason teaches, that man was made to serve and glorify his Creator. And if it be rational to suppose that God immediately communicates himself to man in any affair, it is in this. It is rational to suppose that God would reserve that knowledge and wisdom, that is of such a divine and excellent nature, to be bestowed immediately by himself, and that it should not be left in the power of second causes. Spiritual wisdom and grace is the highest and most excellent gift that ever God bestows on any creature: in this the highest excellency and perfection of a rational creature consists. It is also immensely the most important of all divine gifts: it is that wherein man's happiness consists, and on which his everlasting welfare depends. How rational is it to suppose that God, however he has left meaner goods and lower gifts to second causes, and in some sort in their power, yet should reserve this most excellent, divine, and important of all divine communications, in his own hands, to be bestowed immediately by himself, as a thing too great for second causes to be concerned in! It is rational to suppose, that this blessing should be immediately from God; for there is no gift or benefit that is in itself so nearly related to the divine nature, there is nothing the creature receives that is so much of God, of his nature, so much a participation of the deity: it is a kind of emanation of God's beauty, and is related to God as the light is to the sun. It is therefore congruous and fit, that when it is given of God, it should be nextly from himself, and by himself, according to his own sovereign will.

It is rational to suppose, that it should be beyond a man's power to obtain this knowledge and light by the mere strength of natural reason; for it is not a thing that belongs to reason, to see the beauty and loveliness of spiritual things; it is not a speculative thing, but depends on the sense of the heart. Reason indeed is necessary in order to it, as it is by reason only that we are become the subjects of the means of it; which means I have already shown to be necessary in order to it, though they have no proper causal in the affair. It is by reason that we become possessed of a notion of those doctrines that are the subject matter of this divine light; and reason may many ways be indirectly and remotely an advantage to it. And reason has also to do in the acts that are immediately consequent on this discovery: a seeing the truth of religion from hence, is by reason; though it be but by one step, and the inference be immediate. So reason has to do in that accepting of, and trusting in Christ, that is consequent on it. But if we take reason strictly, not for the faculty of mental perception in general, but for ratiocination, or a power of inferring by arguments; I say, if we take reason thus, the perceiving of spiritual beauty and excellency no more belongs to reason, than it belongs to the sense of feeling to perceive colors, or to the power of seeing to perceive the sweetness of food. It is out of reason's province to perceive the beauty or loveliness of any thing: such a perception does not belong to that faculty. Reason's work is to perceive truth and not excellency. It is not ratiocination that gives men the perception of the beauty and amiableness of a countenance, though it may be many ways indirectly an advantage to it; yet it is no more reason that immediately perceives it, than it is reason that perceives the sweetness of honey: it depends on the sense of the heart. Reason may determine that a countenance is beautiful to others, it may determine that honey is sweet to others; but it will never give me a perception of its sweetness.

I will conclude with a brief improvement of what has been said.

FIRST. This doctrine may lead us to reflect on the goodness of God, that has so ordered it, that a saving evidence of the truth of the gospel is such, as is attainable by persons of mean capacities and advantages, as well as those that are of the greatest parts and learning. If the evidence of the gospel depended only on history, and such reasonings as learned men only are capable of, it would be above the reach of far the greatest part of mankind. But persons with but an ordinary degree of knowledge, are capable, without a long and subtle train of reasoning, to see the divine excellency of the things of religion: they are capable of being taught by the Spirit of God, as well as learned men. The evidence that is this way obtained, is vastly better and more satisfying, than all that can be obtained by the arguings of those that are most learned, and greatest masters of reason. And babes are as capable of knowing these things, as the wise and prudent; and they are often hid from these when they are revealed to those. 1 Cor. i. 26, 27, "For ye see your calling, brethren, how that not many wise men, after the flesh, not many mighty, nor many noble are called. But God hath chosen the foolish things of the world."

SECONDLY. This doctrine may well put us upon examining ourselves, whether we have ever had this divine light, that has been described, let into our souls. If there be such a thing indeed, and it be not only a notion or whimsy of persons of weak and distempered brains, then doubtless it is a thing of great importance, whether we have thus been taught by the Spirit of God; whether the light of the glorious gospel of Christ, who is the image of God, hath shined unto us, giving us the light of the knowledge of the glory of God in the face of Jesus Christ; whether we have seen the Son, and believed on him, or have that faith of gospel doctrines that arises from a spiritual sight of Christ.

THIRDLY. All may hence be exhorted earnestly to seek this spiritual light. To influence and move to it, the following things may be considered.

1. This is the most excellent and divine wisdom that any creature is capable of. It is more excellent than any human learning; it is far more excellent than all the knowledge of the greatest philosophers or statesmen. Yea, the least glimpse of the glory of God in the face of Christ doth more exalt and ennoble the soul, than all the knowledge of those that have the greatest speculative understanding in divinity without grace. This knowledge has the most noble object that is or can be, viz., the divine glory or excellency of God and Christ. The knowledge of these objects is that wherein consists the most excellent knowledge of the angels, yea, of God himself.

2. This knowledge is that which is above all others sweet and joyful. Men have a great deal of pleasure in human knowledge, in studies of natural things; but this is nothing to that joy which arises from this divine light shining into the soul. This light gives a view of those things that are immensely the most exquisitely beautiful, and capable of delighting the eye of the understanding. This spiritual light is the dawning of the light of glory in the heart. There is nothing so powerful as this to support persons in affliction, and to give the mind peace and brightness in this stormy and dark world.

3. This light is such as effectually influences the inclination, and changes the nature of the soul. It assimilates the nature to the divine nature, and changes the soul into an image of the same glory that is beheld. 2 Cor. iii. 18, "But we all with open face, beholding as in a glass the glory of the Lord, are changed into the same image, from glory to glory, even as by the Spirit of the Lord." This knowledge will wean from the world, and raise the inclination to heavenly things. It will turn the heart to God as the fountain of good, and to choose him for the only portion. This light, and this only, will bring the soul to a saving close with Christ. It conforms the heart to the gospel, mortifies its enmity and opposition against the scheme of salvation therein revealed: it causes the heart to embrace the joyful tidings, and entirely to adhere to, and acquiesce in the revelation of Christ as our Savior: it causes the whole soul to accord and symphonize with it, admitting it with entire credit and respect, cleaving to it with full inclination and affection; and it effectually disposes the soul to give up itself entirely to Christ.

4. This light, and this only, has its fruit in a universal holiness of life. No merely notional or speculative understanding of the doctrines of religion will ever bring to this. But this light, as it reaches the bottom of the heart, and changes the nature, so it will effectually dispose to a universal obedience. It shows God's worthiness to be obeyed and served. It draws forth the heart in a sincere love to God, which is the only principle of a true, gracious, and universal obedience; and it convinces of the reality of those glorious rewards that God has promised to them that obey him.

JUSTIFICATION
BY FAITH ALONE

ROMANS iv. 5.—But to him that worketh not, but believeth on him that justifieth the ungodly, his faith is counted for righteousness.

. . . I know there are many that make as though this controversy was of no great importance; that it is chiefly a matter of nice speculation, depending on certain subtle distinctions, which many that make use of them do not understand themselves; and that the difference is not of such consequence as to be worth the being zealous about; and that more hurt is done by raising disputes about it than good.

Indeed I am far from thinking that it is of absolute necessity that persons should understand, and be agreed upon, all the distinctions needful particularly to explain and defend this doctrine against all cavils and objections (though all Christians should strive after an increase of knowledge, and none should content themselves without some clear and distinct understanding in this point): but that we should believe in the general, according to the clear and abundant revelations of God's word, that it is none of our own excellency, virtue, or righteousness, that is the ground of our being received from a state of condemnation into a state of acceptance in God's sight, but only Jesus Christ, and his righteousness, and worthiness, received by faith. This I think to be of great importance, at least in application to ourselves; and that for the following reasons.

1. The Scripture treats of this doctrine, as a doctrine of very great importance. That there is a certain doctrine of justification by faith, in opposition to justification by the works of the law, that the Apostle Paul insists upon as of the greatest importance, none will deny; because there is nothing in the Bible more apparent. The apostle, under the infallible conduct of the Spirit of God, thought it worth his most strenuous and zealous disputing about and defending. He speaks of the contrary doctrine as fatal and ruinous to the souls of men, in the latter end of the ninth chapter of Romans, and beginning of the tenth. He speaks of it as subversive of the gospel of Christ, and calls it another gospel, and says concerning it, if any one, "though an angel from heaven, preach it, let him be accursed"; Gal. i. 6–9 compared with the following part of the epistle. Certainly we must allow the apostles to be good judges of the importance and tendency of doctrines; at least the Holy Ghost in them. And doubtless we are safe, and in no danger of harshness and censoriousness, if we only follow him, and keep close to his express teachings, in what we believe and say of the hurtful and pernicious tendency of any error. Why are we to blame, or to be cried out of, for saying what the Bible has taught us to say, or for believing what the Holy Ghost has taught us to that end that we might believe it?

2. The adverse scheme lays another foundation of man's salvation than God hath laid. I do not now speak of that ineffectual redemption that they suppose to be universal, and what all mankind are equally the subjects of; but I say, it lays entirely another foundation of man's actual, discriminating salvation, or that salvation, wherein true Christians differ from wicked men. We suppose the foundation of this to be Christ's worthiness and righteousness: on the contrary, that scheme supposes it to be men's own virtue; even so, that this is the ground of a saving

interest in Christ itself. It takes away Christ out of the place of the bottom stone, and puts in men's own virtue in the room of him: so that Christ himself in the affair of distinguishing, actual salvation, is laid upon this foundation. And the foundation being so different, I leave it to every one to judge whether the difference between the two schemes consists only in punctilios of small consequence. The foundations being contrary, makes the whole scheme exceeding diverse and opposite; the one is a gospel scheme, the other a legal one.

3. It is in this doctrine that the most essential difference lies between the covenant of grace and the first covenant. The adverse scheme of justification supposes that we are justified by our works, in the very same sense wherein man was to have been justified by his works under the first covenant. By that covenant our first parents were not to have had eternal life given them for any proper merit in their obedience; because their perfect obedience was a debt that they owed God: nor was it to be bestowed for any proportion between the dignity of their obedience, and the value of the reward; but only it was to be bestowed from a regard to a moral fitness in the virtue of their obedience to the reward of God's favor; and a title to eternal life was to be given them, as a testimony of God's pleasedness with their works, or his regard to the inherent beauty of their virtue. And so it is the very same way that those in the adverse scheme suppose that we are received into God's special favor now, and to those saving benefits that are the testimonies of it. I am sensible the divines of that side entirely disclaim the Popish doctrine of merit; and are free to speak of our utter unworthiness, and the great imperfection of all our services: but after all, it is our virtue, imperfect as it is, that recommends men to God, by which good men come to have a saving interest in Christ, and God's respect to their goodness. So that whether they will allow

the term *merit* or no, yet they hold, that we are accepted by our own merit, in the same sense though not in the same degree as under the first covenant.

But the great and most distinguishing difference between that covenant and the covenant of grace is, that by the covenant of grace we are not thus justified by our own works, but only by faith in Jesus Christ. It is on this account chiefly that the new covenant deserves the name of a covenant of grace, as is evident by Rom. iv. 16: "Therefore it is of faith, that it might be by grace." And chap. iii. 20, 24, "Therefore by the deeds of the law, there shall no flesh be justified in his sight—Being justified freely by his grace, through the redemption that is in Jesus Christ." And chap. xi. 6, "And if by grace, then it is no more of works; otherwise grace is no more grace: but if it be of works; then it is no more grace; otherwise work is no more work." Gal. v. 1, "Whosoever of you are justified by the law, ye are fallen from grace." And therefore the apostle, when in the same epistle to the Galatians he speaks of the doctrine of justification by works as another gospel, he adds, "which is not another," chap. i. verses 6, 7. It is no gospel at all; it is law: it is no covenant of grace, but of works: it is not an evangelical, but a legal doctrine. Certainly that doctrine wherein consists the greatest and most essential difference between the covenant of grace and the first covenant, must be a doctrine of great importance. That doctrine of the gospel by which above all others it is worthy of the name gospel, is doubtless a very important doctrine of the gospel.

4. This is the main thing that fallen men stood in need of divine revelation for, to teach us how we that have sinned may come to be again accepted of God; or, which is the same thing, how the sinner may be justified. Something beyond the light of nature is necessary to salvation chiefly on this account. Mere natural reason afforded no means by which we could come to the knowledge of this,

it depending on the sovereign pleasure of the Being that we had offended by sin. This seems to be the great drift of that revelation that God has given, and of all those mysteries it reveals, all those great doctrines that are peculiarly doctrines of revelation, and above the light of nature. It seems to have been very much on this account, that it was requisite that the doctrine of the Trinity itself should be revealed to us; that by a discovery of the concern of the several divine persons in the great affair of our salvation, we might the better understand and see how all our dependence in this affair is on God, and our sufficiency all in him, and not in ourselves; that he is all in all in this business, agreeable to that in 1 Cor. i. 29–31, "That no flesh should glory in his presence. But of him are ye in Christ Jesus, who of God is made unto us wisdom, and righteousness, and sanctification, and redemption: that according as it is written, He that glorieth, let him glory in the Lord." What is the gospel, but only the glad tidings of a new way of acceptance with God unto life, a way wherein sinners may come to be free from the guilt of sin, and obtain a title to eternal life? And if, when this way is revealed, it is rejected, and another of man's devising be put in the room of it, without doubt it must be an error of great importance, and the apostle might well say it was another gospel.

5. The contrary scheme of justification derogates much from the honor of God and the Mediator. I have already shown how it diminishes the glory of the Mediator, in ascribing that to man's virtue and goodness, which belongs alone to his worthiness and righteousness.

By the apostle's sense of the matter it renders Christ needless: Gal. v. 4, "Christ is become of no effect to you, whosoever of you are justified by the law." If that scheme of justification be followed in its consequences, it utterly overthrows the glory of all the great things that have been contrived, and done, and suffered in the work of redemption. Gal. ii. 21, "If righteousness come by the law, Christ is dead in vain." It has also been already shown how it diminishes the glory of divine grace (which is the attribute God hath especially set himself to glorify in the work of redemption); and so that it greatly diminishes the obligation to gratitude in the sinner that is saved: yea, that in the sense of the apostle, it makes void the distinguishing grace of the gospel. Gal. v. 4, "Whosoever of you are justified by the law, ye are fallen from grace." It diminishes the glory of the grace of God and the Redeemer, and proportionably magnifies man. It makes him something before God, when indeed he is nothing: it makes the goodness and excellency of fallen man to be something, which I have shown are nothing. I have also already shown, that it is contrary to the truth of God in the threatening of his holy law, to justify the sinner for his virtue. And whether it were contrary to God's truth or no, it is a scheme of things very unworthy of God, that supposes that God, when about to lift up a poor, forlorn malefactor, condemned to eternal misery for sinning against his Majesty, out of his misery, and to make him unspeakably and eternally happy, by bestowing his Son and himself upon him, as it were, sets all this to sale, for the price of his virtue and excellency. I know that those we oppose do acknowledge, that the price is very disproportionate to the benefit bestowed; and say, that God's grace is wonderfully manifested in accepting so little virtue, and bestowing so glorious a reward for such imperfect righteousness. But seeing we are such infinitely sinful and abominable creatures in God's sight, and by our infinite guilt have brought ourselves into such wretched and deplorable circumstances, and all our righteousnesses are nothing, and ten thousand times worse than nothing (if God looks upon them as they be in themselves), is it not immensely more worthy of the infinite majesty and glory of God, to deliver and make happy such poor, filthy worms, such wretched vagabonds and captives, without any money or price of theirs, or any manner of expectation of any excellency or virtue in them, in any wise to recommend them? Will it not betray a foolish, exalting opinion of ourselves, and a mean one of God, to have a thought of offering any thing of ours, to recommend us to the favor of being brought from wallowing, like filthy swine, in the mire of our sins, and from the enmity and misery of devils in the lowest hell, to the state of God's dear children, in the everlasting arms of his love, in heavenly glory; or to imagine that that is the constitution of God, that we should bring our filthy rags, and offer them to him as the price of this?

6. The opposite scheme does most directly tend to lead men to trust in their own righteousness for justification, which is a thing fatal to the soul. This is what men are of themselves exceedingly prone to do (and that though they are never so much taught the contrary), through the exceeding partial and high thoughts they have of themselves, and their exceeding dulness of apprehending any such mystery as our being accepted for the righteousness of another. But this scheme does directly teach men to trust in their own righteousness for justification; in that it teaches them that this is indeed what they must be justified by, being the way of justification that God himself has appointed. So that if a man had naturally no disposition to trust in his own righteousness, yet if he embraced this scheme, and acted consistent with it, it would lead him to it. . . .

SINNERS IN THE HANDS
OF AN ANGRY GOD

DEUTERONOMY xxxii. 35.—Their foot shall slide in
due time.

In this verse is threatened the vengeance of God on the
wicked unbelieving Israelites, that were God's visible
people, and lived under means of grace; and that notwithstanding all God's wonderful works that he had
wrought towards that people, yet remained, as is expressed verse 28, void of counsel, having no understanding in them; and that, under all the cultivations of
heaven, brought forth bitter and poisonous fruit; as in
the two verses next preceding the text.

The expression that I have chosen for my text, *their
foot shall slide in due time*, seems to imply the following
things relating to the punishment and destruction that
these wicked Israelites were exposed to.

1. That they were always exposed to destruction; as
one that stands or walks in slippery places is always
exposed to fall. This is implied in the manner of their
destruction's coming upon them, being represented by
their foot's sliding. The same is expressed, Psalm lxxiii.
18: "Surely thou didst set them in slippery places; thou
castedst them down into destruction."

2. It implies, that they were always exposed to sudden,
unexpected destruction. As he that walks in slippery
places is every moment liable to fall, he cannot foresee
one moment whether he shall stand or fall the next; and
when he does fall, he falls at once, without warning,

which is also expressed in that Psalm lxxiii. 18, 19: "Surely thou didst set them in slippery places; thou castedst them down into destruction: how are they brought into desolation as in a moment."

3. Another thing implied is, that they are liable to fall of themselves, without being thrown down by the hand of another; as he that stands or walks on slippery ground needs nothing but his own weight to throw him down.

4. That the reason why they are not fallen already, and do not fall now, is only that God's appointed time is not come. For it is said that when that due time, or appointed time comes, *their feet shall slide*. Then they shall be left to fall, as they are inclined by their own weight. God will not hold them up in these slippery places any longer, but will let them go; and then, at that very instant, they shall fall into destruction; as he that stands in such slippery declining ground on the edge of a pit that he cannot stand alone, when he is let go he immediately falls and is lost.

[margin: implications]

The observation from the words that I would now insist upon is this.

There is nothing that keeps wicked men at any one moment out of hell, but the mere pleasure of God.

By the mere pleasure of God, I mean his <u>sovereign</u> pleasure, his <u>arbitrary</u> will, restrained by no obligation, hindered by no manner of difficulty, any more than if nothing else but God's mere will had in the least degree or in any respect whatsoever, any hand in the preservation of wicked men one moment.

The truth of this observation may appear by the following considerations.

1. There is no want of power in God to cast wicked men into hell at any moment. Men's hands cannot be strong when God rises up: the strongest have no power to resist him, nor can any deliver out of his hands.

He is not only able to cast wicked men into hell, but

[margin: Considerations]

he can most easily do it. Sometimes an earthly prince meets with a great deal of difficulty to subdue a rebel, that has found means to fortify himself, and has made himself strong by the number of his followers. But it is not so with God. There is no fortress that is any defence against the power of God. Though hand join in hand, and vast multitudes of God's enemies combine and associate themselves, they are easily broken in pieces: they are as great heaps of light chaff before the whirlwind; or large quantities of dry stubble before devouring flames. We find it easy to tread on and crush a worm that we see crawling on the earth; so it is easy for us to cut or singe a slender thread that any thing hangs by; thus easy is it for God, when he pleases, to cast his enemies down to hell. What are we, that we should think to stand before him, at whose rebuke the earth trembles, and before whom the rocks are thrown down!

2. They deserve to be cast into hell; so that divine justice never stands in the way, it makes no objection against God's using his power at any moment to destroy them. Yea, on the contrary, justice calls aloud for an infinite punishment of their sins. Divine justice says of the tree that brings forth such grapes of Sodom, "Cut it down, why cumbereth it the ground?" Luke xiii. 7. The sword of divine justice is every moment brandished over their heads, and it is nothing but the hand of arbitrary mercy, and God's mere will, that holds it back.

3. They are already under a sentence of condemnation to hell. They do not only justly deserve to be cast down thither, but the sentence of the law of God, that eternal and immutable rule of righteousness that God has fixed between him and mankind, is gone out against them; and stands against them; so that they are bound over already to hell: John iii. 18, "He that believeth not is condemned already." So that every unconverted man properly belongs to hell; that is his place; from thence

he is: John viii. 23, "Ye are from beneath:" and thither he is bound; it is the place that justice, and God's word, and the sentence of his unchangeable law, assign to him.

4. They are now the objects of that very same anger and wrath of God, that is expressed in the torments of hell: and the reason why they do not go down to hell at each moment, is not because God, in whose power they are, is not then very angry with them; as angry, as he is with many of those miserable creatures that he is now tormenting in hell, and do there feel and bear the fierceness of his wrath. Yea, God is a great deal more angry with great numbers that are now on earth; yea, doubtless, with many that are now in this congregation, that, it may be, are at ease and quiet, than he is with many of those that are now in the flames of hell.

So that it is not because God is unmindful of their wickedness, and does not resent it, that he does not let loose his hand and cut them off. God is not altogether such a one as themselves, though they may imagine him to be so. The wrath of God burns against them; their damnation does not slumber; the pit is prepared; the fire is made ready; the furnace is now hot; ready to receive them; the flames do now rage and glow. The glittering sword is whet, and held over them, and the pit hath opened her mouth under them.

5. The devil stands ready to fall upon them, and seize them as his own, at what moment God shall permit him. They belong to him; he has their souls in his possession, and under his dominion. The Scripture represents them as his goods, Luke xi. 21. The devils watch them; they are ever by them, at their right hand; they stand waiting for them, like greedy hungry lions that see their prey, and expect to have it, but are for the present kept back; if God should withdraw his hand by which they are restrained, they would in one moment fly upon their poor souls. The old serpent is gaping for them; hell opens its

mouth wide to receive them; and if God should permit it, they would be hastily swallowed up and lost.

6. There are in the souls of wicked men those hellish principles reigning, that would presently kindle and flame out into hell-fire, if it were not for God's restraints. There is laid in the very nature of carnal men, a foundation for the torments of hell: there are those corrupt principles, in reigning power in them, and in full possession of them, that are the beginnings of hell-fire. These principles are active and powerful, exceeding violent in their nature, and if it were not for the restraining hand of God upon them, they would soon break out, they would flame out after the same manner as the same corruptions, the same enmity does in the hearts of damned souls, and would beget the same torments in them as they do in them. The souls of the wicked are in Scripture compared to the troubled sea, Isaiah lvii. 20. For the present God restrains their wickedness by his mighty power, as he does the raging waves of the troubled sea, saying, "Hitherto shalt thou come, and no further"; but if God should withdraw that restraining power, it would soon carry all before it. Sin is the ruin and misery of the soul; it is destructive in its nature; and if God should leave it without restraint, there would need nothing else to make the soul perfectly miserable. The corruption of the heart of man is a thing that is immoderate and boundless in its fury; and while wicked men live here, it is like fire pent up by God's restraints, whereas if it were let loose, it would set on fire the course of nature; and as the heart is now a sink of sin, so, if sin was not restrained, it would immediately turn the soul into a fiery oven, or a furnace of fire and brimstone.

7. It is no security to wicked men for one moment, that there are no visible means of death at hand. It is no security to a natural man, that he is now in health, and that he does not see which way he should now immedi-

ately go out of the world by any accident, and that there is no visible danger in any respect in his circumstances. The manifold and continual experience of the world in all ages, shows that this is no evidence that a man is not on the very brink of eternity, and that the next step will not be into another world. The unseen, unthought of ways and means of persons' going suddenly out of the world are innumerable and inconceivable. Unconverted men walk over the pit of hell on a rotten covering, and there are innumerable places in this covering so weak that they will not bear their weight, and these places are not seen. The arrows of death fly unseen at noonday; the sharpest sight cannot discern them. God has so many different, unsearchable ways of taking wicked men out of the world and sending them to hell, that there is nothing to make it appear, that God had need to be at the expense of a miracle, or go out of the ordinary course of his providence, to destroy any wicked man, at any moment. All the means that there are of sinners' going out of the world, are so in God's hands, and so absolutely subject to his power and determination, that it does not depend at all less on the mere will of God, whether sinners shall at any moment go to hell, than if means were never made use of, or at all concerned in the case.

8. Natural men's prudence and care to preserve their own lives, or the care of others to preserve them, do not secure them a moment. This, divine providence and universal experience do also bear testimony to. There is this clear evidence that men's own wisdom is no security to them from death; that if it were otherwise we should see some difference between the wise and politic men of the world, and others, with regard to their liableness to early and unexpected death; but how is it in fact? Eccles. ii. 16, "How dieth the wise man? As the fool."

9. All wicked men's pains and contrivance they use to escape hell, while they continue to reject Christ, and so

remain wicked men, do not secure them from hell one moment. Almost every natural man that hears of hell, flatters himself that he shall escape it; he depends upon himself for his own security, he flatters himself that he contrives well for himself, and that his schemes will not fail. They hear indeed that there are but few saved, and that the bigger part of men that have died heretofore are gone to hell; but each one imagines that he lays out matters better for his own escape than others have done: he does not intend to come to that place of torment; he says within himself, that he intends to take care that shall be effectual, and to order matters so for himself as not to fail.

But the foolish children of men do miserably delude themselves in their own schemes, and in their confidence in their own strength and wisdom, they trust to nothing but a shadow. The bigger part of those that heretofore have lived under the same means of grace, and are now dead, are undoubtedly gone to hell; and it was not because they were not as wise as those that are now alive; it was not because they did not lay out matters as well for themselves to secure their own escape. If it were so that we could come to speak with them, and could inquire of them, one by one, whether they expected, when alive, and when they used to hear about hell, ever to be subjects of that misery, we, doubtless, should hear one and another reply, "No, I never intended to come here: I had laid out matters otherwise in my mind; I thought I should contrive well for myself: I thought my scheme good: I intended to take effectual care; but it came upon me unexpectedly; I did not look for it at that time, and in that manner; it came as a thief: death outwitted me: God's wrath was too quick for me: O my cursed foolishness! I was flattering myself, and pleasing myself with vain dreams of what I would do hereafter; and when I was saying peace and safety, then sudden destruction came upon me."

10. God has laid himself under no obligation, by any promise, to keep any natural man out of hell one moment: God certainly has made no promises either of eternal life, or of any deliverance or preservation from eternal death, but what are contained in the covenant of grace, the promises that are given in Christ, in whom all the promises are yea and amen. But surely they have no interest in the promises of the covenant of grace that are not the children of the covenant, and that do not believe in any of the promises of the covenant, and have no interest in the Mediator of the covenant.

So that, whatever some have imagined and pretended about promises made to natural men's earnest seeking and knocking, it is plain and manifest, that whatever pains a natural man takes in religion, whatever prayers he makes, till he believes in Christ, God is under no manner of obligation to keep him a moment from eternal destruction.

So that thus it is, that natural men are held in the hand of God over the pit of hell; they have deserved the fiery pit, and are already sentenced to it; and God is dreadfully provoked, his anger is as great towards them as to those that are actually suffering the executions of the fierceness of his wrath in hell, and they have done nothing in the least, to appease or abate that anger, neither is God in the least bound by any promise to hold them up one moment; the devil is waiting for them, hell is gaping for them, the flames gather and flash about them, and would fain lay hold on them and swallow them up; the fire pent up in their own hearts is struggling to break out; and they have no interest in any Mediator, there are no means within reach that can be any security to them. In short, they have no refuge, nothing to take hold of; all that preserves them every moment is the mere arbitrary will, and uncovenanted, unobliged forbearance of an incensed God.

Application

The use may be of awakening to unconverted persons in this congregation. This that you have heard is the case of every one of you that are out of Christ. That world of misery, that lake of burning brimstone, is extended abroad under you. There is the dreadful pit of the glowing flames of the wrath of God; there is hell's wide gaping mouth open; and you have nothing to stand upon, nor any thing to take hold of. There is nothing between you and hell but the air; it is only the power and mere pleasure of God that holds you up.

You probably are not sensible of this; you find you are kept out of hell, but do not see the hand of God in it; but look at other things, as the good state of your bodily constitution, your care of your own life, and the means you use for your own preservation. But indeed these things are nothing; if God should withdraw his hand, they would avail no more to keep you from falling, than the thin air to hold up a person that is suspended in it.

Your wickedness makes you as it were heavy as lead, and to tend downwards with great weight and pressure towards hell; and if God should let you go, you would immediately sink and swiftly descend and plunge into the bottomless gulf, and your healthy constitution, and your own care and prudence, and best contrivance, and all your righteousness, would have no more influence to uphold you and keep you out of hell, than a spider's web would have to stop a falling rock. Were it not that so is the sovereign pleasure of God, the earth would not bear you one moment; for you are a burden to it; the creation groans with you; the creature is made subject to the bondage of your corruption, not willingly; the sun does not willingly shine upon you to give you light to serve sin and Satan; the earth does not willingly yield her increase to satisfy your lusts; nor is it willingly a stage for your wickedness to be acted upon; the air does not willingly serve you for breath to maintain the flame of life in your vitals, while you spend your life in the service of God's enemies. God's creatures are good, and were made for men to serve God with, and do not willingly subserve to any other purpose, and groan when they are abused to purposes so directly contrary to their nature and end. And the world would spew you out, were it not for the sovereign hand of him who hath subjected it in hope. There are the black clouds of God's wrath now hanging directly over your heads, full of the dreadful storm, and big with thunder; and were it not for the restraining hand of God, it would immediately burst forth upon you. The sovereign pleasure of God, for the present, stays his rough wind; otherwise it would come with fury, and your destruction would come like a whirlwind, and you would be like the chaff of the summer threshing floor.

The wrath of God is like great waters that are dammed for the present; they increase more and more, and rise higher and higher, till an outlet is given; and the longer the stream is stopped, the more rapid and mighty is its course, when once it is let loose. It is true, that judgment against your evil work has not been executed hitherto; the floods of God's vengeance have been withheld; but your guilt in the mean time is constantly increasing, and you are every day treasuring up more wrath; the waters are continually rising, and waxing more and more mighty; and there is nothing but the mere pleasure of God, that holds the waters back, that are unwilling to be stopped, and press hard to go forward. If God should only withdraw his hand from the floodgate, it would immediately fly open, and the fiery floods of the fierceness and wrath of God, would rush forth with inconceivable fury, and would come upon you with omnipotent power; and if your strength were ten thousand times greater than it is, yea, ten thousand times greater than the strength of the stoutest, sturdiest devil in hell it would be nothing to withstand or endure it.

The bow of God's wrath is bent, and the arrow made ready on the string, and justice bends the arrow at your heart, and strains the bow, and it is nothing but the mere pleasure of God, and that of an angry God, without any promise or obligation at all, that keeps the arrow one moment from being made drunk with your blood.

Thus are all you that never passed under a great change of heart, by the mighty power of the Spirit of God upon your souls; all that were never born again, and made new creatures, and raised from being dead in sin, to a state of new, and before altogether unexperienced light and life, (however you may have reformed your life in many things, and may have had religious affections, and may keep up a form of religion in your families and closets, and in the houses of God, and may be strict in it,) you are thus in the hands of an angry God; it is nothing but his mere pleasure that keeps you from being this moment swallowed up in everlasting destruction.

However unconvinced you may now be of the truth of what you hear, by and by you will be fully convinced of it. Those that are gone from being in the like circumstances with you, see that it was so with them; for destruction came suddenly upon most of them; when they expected nothing of it, and while they were saying, Peace and safety: now they see, that those things that they depend on for peace and safety were nothing but thin air and empty shadows.

The God that holds you over the pit of hell, much as one holds a spider, or some loathsome insect, over the fire, abhors you, and is dreadfully provoked; his wrath towards you burns like fire; he looks upon you as worthy of nothing else, but to be cast into the fire; he is of purer eyes than to bear to have you in his sight; you are ten thousand times so abominable in his eyes, as the most hateful and venomous serpent is in ours. You have offended him infinitely more than ever a stubborn rebel did his prince: and yet it is nothing but his hand that holds you from falling into the fire every moment: it is ascribed to nothing else, that you did not go to hell the last night; that you was suffered to awake again in this world, after you closed your eyes to sleep; and there is no other reason to be given, why you have not dropped into hell since you arose in the morning, but that God's hand has held you up: there is no other reason to be given why you have not gone to hell, since you have sat here in the house of God, provoking his pure eyes by your sinful wicked manner of attending his solemn worship: yea, there is nothing else that is to be given as a reason why you do not this very moment drop down into hell.

O sinner! consider the fearful danger you are in: it is a great furnace of wrath, a wide and bottomless pit, full of the fire of wrath, that you are held over in the hand of that God, whose wrath is provoked and incensed as much against you, as against many of the damned in hell: you hang by a slender thread, with the flames of divine wrath flashing about it, and ready every moment to singe it, and burn it asunder; and you have no interest in any Mediator, and nothing to lay hold of to save yourself, nothing to keep off the flames of wrath, nothing of your own, nothing that you ever have done, nothing that you can do, to induce God to spare you one moment.

And consider here more particularly several things concerning that wrath that you are in such danger of.

1. Whose wrath it is. It is the wrath of the infinite God. If it were only the wrath of man, though it were of the most potent prince, it would be comparatively little to be

regarded. The wrath of kings is very much dreaded, especially of absolute monarchs, that have the possessions and lives of their subjects wholly in their power, to be disposed of at their mere will. Prov. xx. 2, "The fear of a king is as the roaring of a lion: whoso provoketh him to anger, sinneth against his own soul." The subject that very much enrages an arbitrary prince, is liable to suffer the most extreme torments that human art can invent, or human power can inflict. But the greatest earthly potentates, in their greatest majesty and strength, and when clothed in their greatest terrors, are but feeble, despicable worms of the dust, in comparison of the great and almighty Creator and King of heaven and earth: it is but little that they can do, when most enraged, and when they have exerted the utmost of their fury. All the kings of the earth before God, are as grasshoppers; they are nothing, and less than nothing: both their love and their hatred is to be despised. The wrath of the great King of kings, is as much more terrible than theirs, as his majesty is greater. Luke xii. 4, 5, "And I say unto you, my friends, Be not afraid of them that kill the body, and after that have no more that they can do. But I will forewarn you whom you shall fear: fear him, which after he hath killed, hath power to cast into hell; yea, I say unto you, Fear him."

2. It is the fierceness of his wrath that you are exposed to. We often read of the fury of God; as in Isaiah lix. 18: "According to their deeds, accordingly he will repay fury to his adversaries." So Isaiah lxvi. 15, "For behold, the Lord will come with fire, and with his chariots like a whirlwind, to render his anger with fury, and his rebuke with flames of fire." And so in many other places. So we read of God's fierceness, Rev. xix. 15. There we read of "the wine-press of the fierceness and wrath of Almighty God." The words are exceedingly terrible: if it had only been said, "the wrath of God," the words would have im-

plied that which is infinitely dreadful: but it is not only said so, but "the fierceness and wrath of God:" the fury of God! the fierceness of Jehovah! Oh how dreadful must that be! Who can utter or conceive what such expressions carry in them! But it is not only said so, but "the fierceness and wrath of Almighty God." As though there would be a very great manifestation of his almighty power in what the fierceness of his wrath should inflict, as though omnipotence should be as it were enraged, and exerted, as men are wont to exert their strength in the fierceness of their wrath. Oh! then, what will be the consequence! What will become of the poor worm that shall suffer it! Whose hands can be strong! And whose heart endure! To what a dreadful, inexpressible, inconceivable depth of misery must the poor creature be sunk who shall be the subject of this!

Consider this, you that are here present, that yet remain in an unregenerate state. That God will execute the fierceness of his anger, implies, that he will inflict wrath without any pity: when God beholds the ineffable extremity of your case, and sees your torment so vastly disproportioned to your strength, and sees how your poor soul is crushed, and sinks down, as it were, into an infinite gloom; he will have no compassion upon you, he will not forbear the executions of his wrath, or in the least lighten his hand; there shall be no moderation or mercy, nor will God then at all stay his rough wind; he will have no regard to your welfare, nor be at all careful lest you should suffer too much in any other sense, than only that you should not suffer beyond what strict justice requires: nothing shall be withheld, because it is so hard for you to bear. Ezek. viii. 18, "Therefore will I also deal in fury; mine eye shall not spare, neither will I have pity; and though they cry in mine ears with a loud voice, yet will I not hear them." Now God stands ready to pity you; this is a day of mercy; you may cry now with some encouragement of obtaining mercy: but when once the day of mercy is past, your most lamentable and dolorous cries and shrieks will be in vain; you will be wholly lost and thrown away of God, as to any regard to your welfare; God will have no other use to put you to, but only to suffer misery; you shall be continued in being to no other end; for you will be a vessel of wrath fitted to destruction; and there will be no other use of this vessel, but only to be filled full of wrath: God will be so far from pitying you when you cry to him, that it is said he will only "laugh and mock," Prov. i. 25, 26, &c.

How awful are those words, Isaiah lxiii. 3, which are the words of the great God: "I will tread them in mine anger, and trample them in my fury, and their blood shall be sprinkled upon my garments, and I will stain all my raiment." It is perhaps impossible to conceive of words that carry in them greater manifestations of these three things, viz., contempt and hatred, and fierceness of indignation. If you cry to God to pity you, he will be so far from pitying you in your doleful case, or showing you the least regard or favor, that instead of that he will only tread you under foot: and though he will know that you cannot bear the weight of omnipotence treading upon you, yet he will not regard that, but he will crush you under his feet without mercy; he will crush out your blood, and make it fly, and it shall be sprinkled on his garments, so as to stain all his raiment. He will not only hate you, but he will have you in the utmost contempt; no place shall be thought fit for you but under his feet, to be trodden down as the mire in the streets.

3. The misery you are exposed to is that which God will inflict to that end, that he might show what that wrath of Jehovah is. God hath had it on his heart to show to angels and men, both how excellent his love is, and also how terrible his wrath is. Sometimes earthly kings have a mind to show how terrible their wrath is, by the

extreme punishments they would execute on those that provoke them. Nebuchadnezzar, that mighty and haughty monarch of the Chaldean empire, was willing to show his wrath when enraged with Shadrach, Meshech, and Abednego; and accordingly gave order that the burning fiery furnace should be heated seven times hotter than it was before; doubtless, it was raised to the utmost degree of fierceness that human art could raise it; but the great God is also willing to show his wrath, and magnify his awful majesty and mighty power in the extreme sufferings of his enemies. Rom. ix. 22, "What if God, willing to show his wrath, and to make his power known, endured with much long-suffering, the vessels of wrath fitted to destruction?" And seeing this is his design, and what he has determined, to show how terrible the unmixed, unrestrained wrath, the fury and fierceness of Jehovah is, he will do it to effect. There will be something accomplished and brought to pass that will be dreadful with a witness. When the great and angry God hath risen up and executed his awful vengeance on the poor sinner, and the wretch is actually suffering the infinite weight and power of his indignation, then will God call upon the whole universe to behold that awful majesty and mighty power that is to be seen in it. Isa. xxxiii. 12, 13, 14, "And the people shall be as the burnings of lime, as thorns cut up shall they be burnt in the fire. Hear, ye that are afar off, what I have done; and ye that are near, acknowledge my might. The sinners in Zion are afraid; fearfulness hath surprised the hypocrites," &c.

Thus it will be with you that are in an unconverted state, if you continue in it; the infinite might, and majesty, and terribleness, of the Omnipotent God shall be magnified upon you in the ineffable strength of your torments: you shall be tormented in the presence of the holy angels, and in the presence of the Lamb; and when you shall be in this state of suffering, the glorious inhabitants of heaven shall go forth and look on the awful spectacle, that they may see what the wrath and fierceness of the Almighty is; and when they have seen it, they will fall down and adore that great power and majesty. Isa. lxvi. 23, 24, "And it shall come to pass, that from one moon to another, and from one Sabbath to another, shall all flesh come to worship before me, saith the Lord. And they shall go forth and look upon the carcasses of the men that have transgressed against me; for their worm shall not die, neither shall their fire be quenched, and they shall be an abhorring unto all flesh."

4. It is everlasting wrath. It would be dreadful to suffer this fierceness and wrath of Almighty God one moment; but you must suffer it to all eternity: there will be no end to this exquisite, horrible misery: when you look forward, you shall see a long forever, a boundless duration before you, which will swallow up your thoughts, and amaze your soul; and you will absolutely despair of ever having any deliverance, any end, any mitigation, any rest at all; you will know certainly that you must wear out long ages, millions of millions of ages, in wrestling and conflicting with this Almighty merciless vengeance; and then when you have so done, when so many ages have actually been spent by you in this manner, you will know that all is but a point to what remains. So that your punishment will indeed be infinite. Oh, who can express what the state of a soul in such circumstances is! All that we can possibly say about it, gives but a very feeble, faint representation of it; it is inexpressible and inconceivable: for "who knows the power of God's anger?"

How dreadful is the state of those that are daily and hourly in danger of this great wrath and infinite misery! But this is the dismal case of every soul in this congregation that has not been born again, however moral and strict, sober and religious, they may otherwise be. Oh that you would consider it, whether you be young or old! There is reason to think, that there are many in this congregation now hearing this discourse, that will actually be the subjects of this very misery to all eternity. We know not who they are, or in what seats they sit, or what thoughts they now have. It may be they are now at ease, and hear all these things without much disturbance, and are now flattering themselves that they are not the persons; promising themselves that they shall escape. If we knew that there was one person, and but one, in the whole congregation, that was to be the subject of this misery, what an awful thing it would be to think of! If we knew who it was, what an awful sight would it be to see such a person! How might all the rest of the congregation lift up a lamentable and bitter cry over him! But alas! Instead of one, how many is it likely will remember this discourse in hell! And it would be a wonder, if some that are now present should not be in hell in a very short time, before this year is out. And it would be no wonder if some persons, that now sit here in some seats of this meeting-house in health, and quiet and secure, should be there before to-morrow morning.

THE EXCELLENCY OF CHRIST

REVELATION v. 5, 6.—And one of the elders saith unto me, Weep not; behold, the Lion of the tribe of Judah, the Root of David, hath prevailed to open the book, and to loose the seven seals thereof. And I beheld, and lo, in the midst of the throne, and of the four beasts, and in the midst of the elders, stood a Lamb as it had been slain—

. . . There is a conjunction of such excellencies in Christ, as, in our manner of conceiving, are very diverse one from another. Such are the various divine perfections and excellencies that Christ is possessed of. Christ is a divine person, or one that is God; and therefore has all the attributes of God. The difference there is between these is chiefly relative, and in our manner of conceiving of them. And those that in this sense are most diverse, do meet in the person of Christ.

I shall mention two instances.

1. There do meet in Jesus Christ infinite highness and infinite condescension. Christ, as he is God, is infinitely great and high above all. He is higher than the kings of the earth: for he is King of kings and Lord of lords. He is higher than the heavens, and higher than the highest angels of heaven. So great is he, that all men, all kings and princes, are as worms of the dust before him; all nations are as the drop of the bucket, and the light dust of the balance; yea, and angels themselves are as nothing before him. He is so high, that he is infinitely above any need of us; above our reach, that we cannot be profitable to him; and above our conceptions, that we cannot com-

prehend him. Prov. xxx. 4, "What is his name, or what is his son's name, if thou canst tell?" Our understandings, if we stretch them never so far, cannot reach up to his divine glory. Job xi. 8, "It is high as heaven, what canst thou do?" Christ is the Creator and great possessor of heaven and earth: he is sovereign Lord of all: he rules over the whole universe, and doth whatsoever pleaseth him: his knowledge is without bound: his wisdom is perfect, and what none can circumvent: his power is infinite, and none can resist him: his riches are immense and inexhaustible: his majesty is infinitely awful.

And yet he is one of infinite condescension. None are so low or inferior, but Christ's condescension is sufficient to take a gracious notice of them. He condescends not only to the angels, humbling himself to behold the things that are done in heaven, but he also condescends to such poor creatures as men; and that not only so as to take notice of princes and great men, but of those that are of meanest rank and degree, the "poor of the world," James ii. 5. Such as are commonly despised by their fellow creatures, Christ does not despise. 1 Cor. i. 28, "Base things of the world, and things that are despised, hath God chosen." Christ condescends to take notice of beggars, Luke xvi. 22, and of servants, and people of the most despised nations: in Christ Jesus is neither "Barbarian, Scythian, bond nor free," Col. iii. 11. He that is thus high, condescends to take a gracious notice of little children. Matt. xix. 14, "Suffer little children to come unto me." Yea, which is much more, his condescension is sufficient to take a gracious notice of the most unworthy, sinful creatures, those that have infinite ill deservings.

Yea, so great is his condescension, that it is not only sufficient to take some gracious notice of such as these, but sufficient for every thing that is an act of condescension. His condescension is great enough to become their friend: it is great enough to become their companion, to unite their souls to him in spiritual marriage: it is great enough to take their nature upon him, to become one of them, that he may be one with them: yea, it is great enough to abase himself yet lower for them, even to expose himself to shame and spitting; yea, to yield up himself to an ignominious death for them. And what act of condescension can be conceived of greater? Yet such an act as this, has his condescension yielded to, for those that are so low and mean, despicable and unworthy!

Such a conjunction of such infinite highness and low condescension, in the same person, is admirable. We see, by manifold instances, what a tendency a high station has in men, to make them to be of a quite a contrary disposition. If one worm be a little exalted above another, by having more dust, or a bigger dunghill, how much does he make of himself! What a distance does he keep from those that are below him! And a little condescension is what he expects should be made much of, and greatly acknowledged. Christ condescends to wash our feet; but how would great men (or rather the bigger worms) account themselves debased by acts of far less condescension!

2. There meet in Jesus Christ, infinite justice and infinite grace. As Christ is a divine person he is infinitely holy and just, infinitely hating sin, and disposed to execute condign punishment for sin. He is the Judge of the world, and is the infinitely just judge of it, and will not at all acquit the wicked, or by any means clear the guilty.

And yet he is one that is infinitely gracious and merciful. Though his justice be so strict with respect to all sin, and every breach of the law, yet he has grace sufficient for every sinner, and even the chief of sinners. And it is not only sufficient for the most unworthy to show them mercy, and bestow some good upon them, and to do all things for them. There is no benefit or blessing that they can receive so great, but the grace of Christ is sufficient to bestow it on the greatest sinner that ever lived. And not only so, but so great is his grace, that nothing is too much as the means of this good: it is sufficient not only to do great things, but also to suffer in order to it; and not only to suffer, but to suffer most extremely even unto death, the most terrible of natural evils; and not only death, but the most ignominious and tormenting, and every way the most terrible death that men could inflict; yea, and greater sufferings than men could inflict, who could only torment the body, but also those sufferings in his soul, that were the more immediate fruits of the wrath of God against the sins of those he undertakes for. . . .

Application

I. From this doctrine we may learn one reason why Christ is called by such a variety of names, and held forth under such a variety of representations in Scripture. It is the better to signify and exhibit to us that variety of excellencies that meet together, and are conjoined in him. Many appellations are mentioned together in one verse: Isa. ix. 6, "For unto us a Child is born, unto us a Son is given, and the government shall be upon his shoulder; and his name shall be called Wonderful, Counsellor, the mighty God, the everlasting Father," without a beginning or end; that he should be a Child, and yet be he whose name is Counsellor, and the mighty God; and well may his name in whom such things are conjoined, be called Wonderful.

By reason of the same wonderful conjunction, Christ is represented by a great variety of sensible things, that are on some account excellent. Thus in some places he is called a Sun, as Mal. iv. 2, in others a Star, Numb. xxiv. 17. And he is especially represented by the Morning Star, as being that which excels all other stars in brightness, and is the forerunner of the day, Rev. xxii. 16. And, as in our text, he is compared to a lion in one verse, and a lamb in the next, so sometimes he is compared to a roe, or a young hart, another creature most diverse from a lion. So in some places he is called a rock, in others he is compared to a pearl: in some places he is called a man of war, and the Captain of our salvation, in other places he is represented as a bridegroom. In the second chapter of Canticles, the 1st verse, he is compared to a rose and lily, that are sweet and beautiful flowers; in the next verse but one, he is compared to a tree, bearing sweet fruit. In Isa. liii. 2, he is called a Root out of a dry ground; but elsewhere, instead of that, he is called the Tree of Life, that grows (not in a dry or barren ground, but) "in the midst of the paradise of God," Rev. ii. 7.

II. Let the consideration of this wonderful meeting of diverse excellencies in Christ induce you to accept him, and close with him as your Saviour. As all manner of excellencies meet in him, so there are concurring in him all manner of arguments and motives, to move you to choose him for your Saviour, and every thing that tends to encourage poor sinners to come and put their trust in him. His fulness and all-sufficiency as a Saviour gloriously appear in that variety of excellencies that has been spoken of.

Fallen man is in a state of exceeding great misery, and is helpless in it, he is a poor weak creature, like an infant, cast out in its blood, in the day that it is born: but Christ is *the Lion of the tribe of Judah*; he is strong, though we are weak; he hath prevailed to do that for us which no creature else could do. Fallen man is a mean, despicable creature, a contemptible worm; but Christ who has undertaken for us, is infinitely honorable and worthy. Fallen man is polluted, but Christ is infinitely holy: fallen man is hateful, but Christ is infinitely dear to him: we have dreadfully provoked God, but Christ has performed that righteousness that is infinitely precious in God's eyes.

And here is not only infinite strength and infinite worthiness, but infinite condescension; and love and mercy, as great as power and dignity: if you are a poor, distressed sinner, whose heart is ready to sink for fear that God never will have mercy on you, you need not be afraid to go to Christ, for fear that he is either unable or unwilling to help you; here is a strong foundation, and an inexhaustible treasure, to answer the necessities of your poor soul; and here is infinite grace and gentleness to invite and embolden a poor, unworthy, fearful soul to come to it. If Christ accepts you, you need not fear but that you will be safe; for he is a strong lion for your defence: and if you come, you need not fear but that you shall be accepted; for he is like a lamb to all that come to him, and receives them with infinite grace and tenderness. It is true he has awful majesty; he is the great God, and is infinitely high above you; but there is this to encourage and embolden the poor sinner, that Christ is a man as well as God; he is a creature as well as the Creator; and he is the most humble and lowly in heart of any creature in heaven or earth. This may well make the poor unworthy creature bold in coming to him. You need not hesitate one moment; but may run to him, and cast yourself upon him; you will certainly be graciously and meekly received by him. Though he be a lion, he will only be a lion to your enemies, but he will be a lamb to you. It could not have been conceived, had it not been so in the person of Christ, that there could have been so much in any Saviour, that is inviting, and tending to encourage sinners to trust in him. Whatever your circumstances are, you need not be afraid to come to such a Saviour as this: be you never so wicked a creature, here is worthiness enough: be you never so poor, and mean, and ignorant a creature, there is no danger of being despised; for though he be so much greater than you, he is also immensely more humble than you. Any one of you that is a father or mother, will not despise one of your own children that comes to you in distress; much less danger is there of Christ despising you, if you in your heart come to him.—Here let me a little expostulate with the poor, burdened, distressed soul.

What are you afraid of, that you dare not venture your soul upon Christ? Are you afraid that he cannot save you; that he is not strong enough to conquer the enemies of your soul? But how can you desire one stronger than the "mighty God?" as Christ is called, Isa. ix. 6. Is there need of greater than infinite strength? Are you afraid that he will not be willing to stoop so low as to take any gracious notice of you? But then, look on him, as he stood in the ring of soldiers, exposing his blessed face to be buffeted and spit upon by them! Behold him bound, with his back uncovered to those that smote him! And behold him hanging on the cross! Do you think that he that had condescension enough to stoop to these things, and that for his crucifiers, will be unwilling to accept you if you come to him? Or, are you afraid, that if he does accept you, that God the Father will not accept him for you? But consider, will God reject his own Son, in whom his infinite delight is and has been, from all eternity, and that is so united to him, that if he should reject him, he would reject himself?

What is there that you can desire should be in a Saviour, that is not in Christ? Or, wherein should you desire a Saviour should be otherwise than Christ is? What excellency is there wanting? What is there that is great or good? What is there that is venerable or winning? What is there that is adorable or endearing? Or, what can you think of, that would be encouraging, that is not to be found in the person of Christ? Would you have your Saviour to be great and honorable, because you are not willing to be beholden to a mean person? And is not Christ a person honorable enough to be worthy that you should be dependent on him? Is he not a person high enough to be worthy to be appointed to so honorable a work as your salvation? Would you not only have a Saviour that is of high degree, but would you have him, notwithstanding his exaltation and dignity, to be made also of low degree, that he might have experience of afflictions and trials, that he might learn by the things that he has suffered, to pity them that suffer and are tempted? And has not Christ been made low enough for you? And has he not suffered enough? Would you not only have him have experience of the afflictions you now suffer, but also of that amazing wrath that you fear hereafter, that he may know how to pity those that are in danger of it, and afraid of it? This Christ has had experience of, which experience gave him a greater sense of it, a thousand times, than you have, or any man living has. Would you have your Saviour to be one that is near to God, that so his mediation might be prevalent with him? And can you desire him to be nearer to God than Christ is, who is his only begotten Son, of the same essence with the Father? And would you not only have him near to God, but also near to you, that you may have free access to him? And would you have him nearer to you than to be in the same nature, and not only so, but united to you by a spiritual union, so close as to be fitly represented by the union of the wife to the husband, of the branch to the vine, of the member to the head; yea, so as to be looked upon as one, and called one spirit? For so he will be united to you, if you accept him. Would you have a Saviour that has given some great and extraordinary testimony of mercy and love to sinners, by something that he has done, as well as by what he says? And can you think or conceive of greater things than Christ has done? Was it not a great thing for him, who was God, to take upon him human nature; to be not only God, but man thenceforward to all eternity? But would you look upon suffering for sinners to be a yet greater testimony of love to sinners, than merely doing, though it be never so extraordinary a thing that he has done? And would you desire that a Saviour should suffer more than Christ has suffered for sinners? What is there wanting, or what would you add if you could, to make him more fit to be your Saviour?

But further, to induce you to accept of Christ as your Saviour, consider two things particularly.

1. How much Christ appears as the Lamb of God in his invitations to you to come to him and trust in him. With what sweet grace and kindness does he from time to time call and invite you; as Prov. viii. 4: "Unto you, O men, I call, and my voice is to the sons of men." And Isa. lv. 1–3, "Ho, every one that thirsteth, come ye to the waters, and he that hath no money; come ye, buy and eat, yea, come, buy wine and milk without money and without price." How graciously is he here inviting every one that thirsts, and in so repeating his invitation over and over, "Come ye to the waters; come, buy and eat, yea, come!" And in declaring the excellency of that entertainment which he invites you to accept of, "Come, buy wine and milk"; and in assuring you that your poverty, and having nothing to pay for it, shall be no objection, "Come, he that hath no money, come without money and without price!" And in the gracious arguments and expostulations that he uses with you! As it follows, "Wherefore do ye spend money for that which is not bread? And your labor for that which satisfieth not? Hearken diligently unto me, and eat ye that which is good, and let your soul delight itself in fatness." As much as to say, "It is altogether needless for you to continue laboring and toiling for that which can never serve your turn, seeking rest in the world and in your own righteousness: I have made abundant provision for you, of that which is really good, and will fully satisfy your desires, and answer your

end, and stand ready to accept of you: you need not be afraid; if you will come to me, I will engage to see all your wants supplied, and you made a happy creature." As he promises in the third verse, "Incline your ear, and come unto me: hear, and your soul shall live, and I will make an everlasting covenant with you, even the sure mercies of David." And so, Prov. ix. at the beginning. How gracious and sweet is the invitation there! "Whoso is simple, let him turn in hither"; let you be never so poor, ignorant, and blind a creature, you shall be welcome. And in the following words, Christ sets forth the provision that he has made for you: "Come, eat of my bread, and drink of the wine which I have mingled." You are in a poor famishing state, and have nothing wherewith to feed your perishing soul; you have been seeking something, but yet remain destitute: hearken, how Christ calls you to eat of his bread, and to drink of the wine that he hath mingled! And how much like a lamb does Christ appear in Matt. xi. 28–30: "Come unto me, all ye that labor, and are heavy laden, and I will give you rest. Take my yoke upon you, and learn of me, for I am meek and lowly in heart; and ye shall find rest to your souls. For my yoke is easy, and my burden is light." O thou poor distressed soul, whoever thou art, that art afraid that you never shall be saved, consider that this that Christ mentions is your very case, when he calls to them that labor, and are heavy laden! And how he repeatedly promises you rest if you come to him! In the 28th verse he says, "I will give you rest." And in the 29th verse, "Ye shall find rest to your souls." This is what you want. This is the thing you have been so long in vain seeking after. O how sweet would rest be to you, if you could but obtain it! Come to Christ, and you shall obtain it. And hear how Christ, to encourage you, represents himself as a lamb! He tells you, that he is meek and lowly in heart; and are you afraid to come to such a one? And again,

Rev. iii. 20, "Behold, I stand at the door and knock: if any man hear my voice, and open the door, I will come in to him, and will sup with him, and he with me." Christ condescends not only to call you to him, but he comes to you; he comes to your door, and there knocks. He might send an officer and seize you as a rebel and vile malefactor; but instead of that, he comes and knocks at your door, and seeks that you would receive him into your house, as your friend and Saviour. And he not only knocks at your door, but he stands there waiting, while you are backward and unwilling. And not only so, but he makes promises what he will do for you, if you will admit him, what privileges he will admit you to; he will "sup with you and you with him." And again, Rev. xxii. 16, 17, "I am the root and the offspring of David, and the bright and morning star. And the Spirit and the bride say, Come: and let him that heareth, say, Come: and let him that is athirst come: and whosoever will, let him come and take of the water of life freely." How does Christ here graciously set before you his own winning, attractive excellency! And how does he condescend to declare to you not only his own invitation, but the invitation of the Spirit and the bride, if by any means he might encourage you to come! And how does he invite every one that will, that they may "take of the water of life freely," that they may take it a free gift, however precious it be, and though it be the water of life!

2. If you do come to Christ, he will appear as a lion, in his glorious power and dominion, to defend you. All those excellencies of his, in which he appears as a lion, shall be yours, and shall be employed for you in your defence, for your safety, and to promote your glory; he will be as a lion to fight against your enemies: he that touches you, or offends you, will provoke his wrath, as he that stirs up a lion. Unless your enemies can conquer this lion, they shall not be able to destroy or hurt you;

unless they are stronger than he, they shall not be able to hinder your happiness. Isa. xxxi. 4, "For thus hath the Lord spoken unto me, Like as the lion and the young lion roaring on his prey, when a multitude of shepherds is called forth against him, he will not be afraid of their voice, nor abase himself for the noise of them; so shall the Lord of hosts come down to fight for mount Zion, and for the hill thereof."

THE PEACE WHICH CHRIST
GIVES HIS TRUE FOLLOWERS

JOHN xiv. 27.—Peace I leave with you, my peace I
give unto you: not as the world giveth, give I unto you.

. . . This legacy of Christ to his true disciples is very
diverse from all that the men of this world ever leave to
their children when they die. The men of this world,
many of them, when they come to die, have great estates
to bequeath to their children, an abundance of the good
things of this world, large tracts of ground, perhaps in a
fruitful soil, covered with flocks and herds. They sometimes leave to their children stately mansions, and vast
treasures of silver, gold, jewels, and precious things,
fetched from both the Indies, and from every side of the
globe of the earth. They leave them wherewith to live in
much state and magnificence, and make a great show
among men, to fare very sumptuously, and swim in
worldly pleasures. Some have crowns, sceptres, and pal-
aces, and great monarchies to leave to their heirs. But
none of these things are to be compared to that blessed
peace of Christ which he has bequeathed to his true
followers. These things are such as God commonly, in
his providence, gives his worst enemies, those whom he
hates and despises most. But Christ's peace is a precious
benefit, which he reserves for his peculiar favorites.
These worldly things, even the best of them, that the
men and princes of the world leave for their children,
are things which God in his providence throws out to
those whom he looks on as dogs; but Christ's peace is the

bread of his children. All these earthly things are but empty shadows, which, however men set their hearts upon them, are not bread, and can never satisfy their souls; but this peace of Christ is a truly substantial, satisfying food, Isai. lv. 2. None of those things if men have them to the best advantage, and in ever so great abundance, can give true peace and rest to the soul, as is abundantly manifest not only in reason, but experience; it being found in all ages, that those who have the most of them, have commonly the least quietness of mind. It is true, there may be a kind of quietness, a false peace they may have in their enjoyment of worldly things; men may bless their souls, and think themselves the only happy persons, and despise others; may say to their souls, as the rich man did, Luke xii. 19, "Soul, thou hast much goods laid up for many years, take thine ease, eat, drink, and be merry." But Christ's peace, which he gives to his true disciples, vastly differs from this peace that men may have in the enjoyments of the world, in the following respects:

1. Christ's peace is a reasonable peace and rest of soul; it is what has its foundation in light and knowledge, in the proper exercises of reason, and a right view of things; whereas the peace of the world is founded in blindness and delusion. The peace that the people of Christ have, arises from their having their eyes open, and seeing things as they be. The more they consider, and the more they know of the truth and reality of things, the more they know what is true concerning themselves, the state and condition they are in; the more they know of God, and the more certain they are that there is a God, and the more they know what manner of being he is, the more certain they are of another world and future judgment, and of the truth of God's threatenings and promises; the more their consciences are awakened and enlightened, and the brighter and the more searching the light is that

they see things in, the more is their peace established: whereas, on the contrary, the peace that the men of the world have in their worldly enjoyments can subsist no otherwise than by their being kept in ignorance. They must be blindfolded and deceived, otherwise they can have no peace: do but let light in upon their consciences, so that they may look about them and see what they are, and what circumstances they are in, and it will at once destroy all their quietness and comfort. Their peace can live nowhere but in the dark. Light turns their ease into torment. The more they know what is true concerning God and concerning themselves, the more they are sensible of the truth concerning those enjoyments which they possess; and the more they are sensible what things now are, and what things are like to be hereafter, the more will their calm be turned into a storm. The worldly man's peace cannot be maintained but by avoiding consideration and reflection. If he allows himself to think, and properly to exercise his reason, it destroys his quietness and comfort. If he would establish his carnal peace, it concerns him to put out the light of his mind, and turn beast as fast as he can. The faculty of reason, if at liberty, proves a mortal enemy to his peace. It concerns him, if he would keep alive his peace, to contrive all ways that may be, to stupefy his mind and deceive himself, and to imagine things to be otherwise than they be. But with respect to the peace which Christ gives, reason is its great friend. The more this faculty is exercised, the more it is established. The more they consider and view things with truth and exactness, the firmer is their comfort, and the higher their joy. How vast a difference is there between the peace of a Christian and the worldling! How miserable are they who cannot enjoy peace any otherwise than by hiding their eyes from the light, and confining themselves to darkness; whose peace is properly stupidity; as the ease that a man has who has taken a dose of stupefying poison, and the ease and pleasure that a drunkard may have in a house on fire over his head, or the joy of a distracted man in thinking that he is a king, though a miserable wretch confined in bedlam: whereas, the peace which Christ gives his true disciples, is the light of life, something of the tranquillity of heaven, the peace of the celestial paradise, that has the glory of God to lighten it.

2. Christ's peace is a virtuous and holy peace. The peace that the men of the world enjoy is vicious; it is a vile stupidity, that depraves and debases the mind, and makes men brutish. But the peace that the saints enjoy in Christ, is not only their comfort, but it is a part of their beauty and dignity. The Christian tranquillity, rest, and joy of real saints, are not only unspeakable privileges, but they are virtues and graces of God's Spirit, wherein the image of God in them does partly consist. This peace has its source in those principles that are in the highest degree virtuous and amiable, such as poverty of spirit, holy resignation, trust in God, divine love, meekness, and charity; the exercise of such blessed fruits of the Spirit as are spoken of, Gal. v. 22, 23.

3. This peace greatly differs from that which is enjoyed by the men of the world, with regard to its exquisite sweetness. It is a peace that passes all that natural men enjoy in worldly things so much, that it passes their understanding and conception, Phil. iv. 7. It is exquisitely sweet, because it has so firm a foundation as the everlasting rock that never can be moved. It is sweet, because perfectly agreeable to reason. It is sweet, because it rises from holy and divine principles, that as they are the virtue, so they are the proper happiness of men.

It is exquisitely sweet, because of the greatness of the objective good that the saints enjoy, and have peace and rest in, being no other than the infinite bounty and fulness of that God who is the fountain of all good. It is sweet, on account of the fulness and perfection of that provision that is made for it in Christ and the new covenant, where there is a foundation laid for the saints' perfect peace; and hereafter they shall actually enjoy perfect peace; and though their peace is not now perfect, it is not owing to any defect in the provision made, but in their own imperfection and misery, sin and darkness; and because as yet they do partly cleave to the world and seek peace from thence, and do not perfectly cleave to Christ. But the more they do so, and the more they see of the provision there is made, and accept of it, and cleave to that alone, the nearer are they brought to perfect tranquillity, Isaiah xxvi. 5.

4. The peace of the Christian infinitely differs from that of the worldling, in that it is unfailing and eternal peace. That peace which carnal men have in the things of the world, is, according to the foundation that it is built upon, of short continuance; like the comfort of a dream, 1 John ii. 17, I Cor. vii. 31. These things, the best and most durable of them, are like bubbles on the face of the water; they vanish in a moment, Hos. x. 7.

But the foundation of the Christian's peace is everlasting; it is what no time, no change, can destroy. It will remain when the body dies; it will remain when the mountains depart and the hills shall be removed, and when the heavens shall be rolled together as a scroll. The fountain of his comfort shall never be diminished, and the stream shall never be dried. His comfort and joy is a living spring in the soul, a well of water springing up to everlasting life.

Application

The use that I would make of this doctrine, is to improve it, as an inducement unto all to forsake the world, no longer seeking peace and rest in its vanities, and to cleave to Christ and follow him. Happiness and rest are what all men are in pursuit of. But the things of the world, wherein most men seek it, can never afford it; they are laboring and spending themselves in vain. But Christ invites you to come to him, and offers you this peace which he gives his true followers, that so much excels all that the world can afford, Isa. lv. 2, 3.

You that have hitherto spent your time in the pursuit of satisfaction and peace in the profit and glory of the world, or in the pleasures and vanities of youth, have this day an offer made to you of that excellent and everlasting peace and blessedness, which Christ has purchased with the price of his own blood, and bestows only on those that are his peculiar favorites, his redeemed ones, that are his portion and treasure, the objects of his everlasting love. As long as you continue to reject those offers and invitations of Christ, and continue in a Christless condition, you never will enjoy any true peace or comfort; but in whatever circumstances you are, you will be miserable; you will be like the prodigal, that in vain endeavored to fill his belly with the husks that the swine did eat: the wrath of God will abide upon, and misery will attend you wherever you go, which you never will, by any means, be able to escape. Christ gives peace to the most sinful and miserable that come to him. He heals the broken in heart and bindeth up their wounds. But it is impossible that they should have peace, that continue in their sins, Isa. lvii. 19–21. There is no peace between God and them; as they have the guilt of sin remaining in their souls, and are under the dominion of sin, so God's indignation continually burns against them, and therefore there is reason why they should travail in pain all their days.

While you continue in such a state, you live in a state of dreadful uncertainty what will become of you, and in continual danger. When you are in the enjoyment of things that are the most pleasing to you, where your heart is best suited, and most cheerful, yet you are in a state of condemnation, hanging over the infernal pit, with the sword of divine vengeance hanging over your head, having no security one moment from utter and remediless destruction. What reasonable peace can any one enjoy in such a state as this? What does it signify to take such a one and clothe him in gorgeous apparel, or to set him on a throne, or at a prince's table, and feed him with the rarest dainties the earth affords? And how miserable is the ease and cheerfulness that such have! What a poor kind of comfort and joy is it that such take in their wealth and pleasures for a moment, while they are the prisoners of divine justice, and wretched captives of the devil, and have none to befriend them or defend them, being without Christ, aliens from the commonwealth of Israel, strangers from the covenant of promise, having no hope, and without God in the world!

I invite you now to a better portion. There are better things provided for the sinful miserable children of men. There is a surer comfort and more durable peace: comfort that you may enjoy in a state of safety and on a sure foundation: a peace and rest that you may enjoy with reason and with your eyes open; having all your sins forgiven, your greatest and most aggravated transgressions blotted out as a cloud, and buried as in the depths of the sea, that they may never be found more; and being not only forgiven, but accepted to favor; being the objects of God's complacence and delight; being taken into God's family and made his children; and having good evidence that your names were written on the heart of Christ before the world was made, and that you have an interest in that covenant of grace that is well ordered in all things and sure; wherein is promised no less than life and immortality, an inheritance incorruptible and undefiled, a crown of glory that fades not away; being in such circumstances, that nothing shall be able to prevent your being happy to all eternity; having for the foundation of your hope, that love of God which is from eternity unto eternity; and his promise and oath, and his omnipotent power, things infinitely firmer than mountains of brass. The mountains shall depart, and the hills be removed, yea, the heavens shall vanish away like smoke, and the earth shall wax old like a garment, yet these things will never be abolished.

In such a state as this you will have a foundation of peace and rest through all changes, and in times of the greatest uproar and outward calamity be defended from all storms, and dwell above the floods, Psalm xxxii. 6, 7; and you shall be at peace with every thing, and God will make all his creatures throughout all parts of his dominion, to befriend you, Job v. 19, 24. You need not be afraid of any thing that your enemies can do unto you, Psalm iii. 5, 6. Those things that now are most terrible to you, viz., death, judgment, and eternity, will then be most comfortable, the most sweet and pleasant objects of your contemplation, at least there will be reason that they should be so. Hearken therefore to the friendly counsel that is given you this day, turn your feet into the way of peace, forsake the foolish and live; forsake those things which are no other than the devil's baits, and seek after this excellent peace and rest of Jesus Christ, that peace of God which passes all understanding. Taste and see; never was any disappointed that made a trial, Prov. xxiv. 13, 14. You will not only find those spiritual comforts that Christ offers you to be of a surpassing sweetness for the present, but they will be to your soul as the dawning light that shines more and more to the perfect day; and the issue of all will be your arrival in heaven, that land of rest, those regions of everlasting joy, where your peace and happiness will be perfect, without the least mixture of trouble or affliction, and never be interrupted nor have an end.

A FAREWELL SERMON

(1750)

2 CORINTHIANS i. 14.—As also you have acknowledged us in part, that we are your rejoicing, even as ye
also are ours in the day of the Lord Jesus.

. . . There are two things which I would now observe:

1. The mutual concerns of ministers and their people
are of the greatest importance.

The Scripture declares, that God will bring every work
into judgment with every secret thing, whether it be good
or whether it be evil. It is fit that all the concerns, and
all the behavior of mankind, both public and private,
should be brought at last before God's tribunal, and
finally determined by an infallible Judge: but it is especially requisite that it should be thus, as to affairs of very
great importance.

Now the mutual concerns of a Christian minister and
his church and congregation, are of the vastest importance: in many respects, of much greater moment than
the temporal concerns of the greatest earthly monarchs,
and their kingdoms or empires. It is of vast consequence
how ministers discharge their office, and conduct themselves towards their people in the work of the ministry,
and in affairs appertaining to it. It is also a matter of vast
importance, how a people receive and entertain a faithful
minister of Christ, and what improvement they make of
his ministry. These things have a more immediate and
direct respect to the great and last end for which man
was made, and the eternal welfare of mankind, than any
of the temporal concerns of men, whether public or pri-

134

vate. And therefore it is especially fit that these affairs should be brought into judgment and openly determined and settled in truth and righteousness; and that to this end, ministers and their people should meet together before the omniscient and infallible judge.

2. The mutual concerns of ministers and their people have a special relation to the main things appertaining to the day of judgment.

They have a special relation to that great and divine person who will then appear as Judge. Ministers are his messengers, sent forth by him; and, in their office and administrations among their people, represent his person, stand in his stead, as those that are sent to declare his mind, to do his work, and to speak and act in his name. And therefore it is especially fit that they should return to him to give an account of their work and success. The king is judge of all his subjects, they are all accountable to him. But it is more especially requisite that the king's ministers, who are especially intrusted with the administrations of his kingdom, and that are sent forth on some special negotiation, should return to him, to give an account of themselves, and their discharge of their trust, and the reception they have met with.

Ministers are not only messengers of the person who at the last day will appear as Judge, but the errand they are sent upon, and the affairs they have committed to them as his ministers, do most immediately concern his honor, and the interest of his kingdom. The work they are sent upon is to promote the designs of his administration and government; and therefore their business with their people has a near relation to the day of judgment; for the great end of that day is completely to settle and establish the affairs of his kingdom, to adjust all things that pertain to it, that every thing that is opposite to the interests of his kingdom may be removed, and that every thing which contributes to the completeness and glory of it may be perfected and confirmed, that this great King may receive his due honor and glory.

Again, the mutual concerns of ministers and their people have a direct relation to the concerns of the day of judgment, as the business of ministers with their people is to promote the eternal salvation of the souls of men, and their escape from eternal damnation; and the day of judgment is the day appointed for that end, openly to decide and settle men's eternal state, to fix some in a state of eternal salvation, and to bring their salvation to its utmost consummation, and to fix others in a state of everlasting damnation and most perfect misery. The mutual concerns of ministers and people have a most direct relation to the day of judgment, as the very design of the work of the ministry is the people's preparation for that day. Ministers are sent to warn them of the approach of that day, to forewarn them of the dreadful sentence then to be pronounced on the wicked, and declare to them the blessed sentence then to be pronounced on the righteous, and to use means with them that they may escape the wrath which is then to come on the ungodly, and obtain the reward then to be bestowed on the saints.

And as the mutual concerns of ministers and their people have so near and direct a relation to that day, it is especially fit that those concerns should be brought in to that day, and there settled and issued; and that in order to this, ministers and their people should meet and appear together before the great Judge at that day.

Application

The improvement I would make of the things which have been observed, is to lead the people here present who have been under my pastoral care, to some reflections, and give them some advice suitable to our present circumstances; relating to what has been lately done in order to our being separated, as to the relation we have heretofore stood in one to another; but expecting to meet each other before the great tribunal at the day of judgment.

The deep and serious consideration of that our future most solemn meeting, is certainly most suitable at such a time as this; there having so lately been that done, which, in all probability, will (as to the relation we have heretofore stood in) be followed with an everlasting separation.

How often have we met together in the house of God in this relation! How often have I spoke to you, instructed, counselled, warned, directed, and fed you, and administered ordinances among you, as the people which were committed to my care, and whose precious souls I had the charge of! But in all probability this never will be again.

The prophet Jeremiah, chap. xxv. 3, puts the people in mind how long he had labored among them in the work of the ministry: "From the thirteenth year of Josiah, the son of Amon, king of Judah, even unto this day (that is, the three and twentieth year), the word of the Lord came unto me, and I have spoken unto you, rising early and speaking." I am not about to compare myself with the prophet Jeremiah; but in this respect I can say as he did, that "I have spoken the word of God to you, unto the three and twentieth year, rising early and speaking." It was three and twenty years, the 15th day of last February, since I have labored in the work of the ministry, in the relation of a pastor to this church and congregation. And though my strength has been weakness, having always labored under great infirmity of body, besides my insufficiency for so great a charge in other respects, yet I have not spared my feeble strength, but have exerted it for the good of your souls. I can appeal to you as the apostle does to his hearers, Gal. iv. 13, "Ye know how through infirmity of the flesh, I preached the gospel unto you." I have spent the prime of my life and strength in labors for your eternal welfare. You are my witnesses, that what strength I have had I have not neglected in idleness, nor laid out in prosecuting worldly schemes, and managing temporal affairs, for the advancement of my outward estate, and aggrandizing myself and family; but have given myself wholly to the work of the ministry, laboring in it night and day, rising early and applying myself to this great business to which Christ appointed me. I have found the work of the ministry among you to be a great work indeed, a work of exceeding care, labor and difficulty: many have been the heavy burdens that I have borne in it, which my strength has been very unequal to. God called me to bear these burdens; and I bless his name, that he has so supported me as to keep me from sinking under them, and that his power herein has been manifested in my weakness; so that although I have often been troubled on every side, yet I have not been distressed; perplexed, but not in despair; cast down, but not destroyed.

But now I have reason to think my work is finished which I had to do as your minister: you have publicly rejected me, and my opportunities cease.

How highly therefore does it now become us to consider of that time when we must meet one another before the chief Shepherd? When I must give an account of my stewardship, of the service I have done for, and the reception and treatment I have had among the people he sent me to: and you must give an account of your own conduct towards me, and the improvement you have made of these three and twenty years of my ministry. For then both you and I must appear together, and we both must give an account, in order to an infallible, righteous and eternal sentence to be passed upon us, by him who will judge us with respect to all that we have said or done in our meeting here, all our conduct one towards another, in the house of God, and elsewhere, on Sabbath days, and on other days; who will try our hearts and manifest our thoughts, and the principles and frames of our minds, will judge us with respect to all the controversies which have subsisted between us, with the strictest impartiality, and will examine our treatment of each other in those controversies: there is nothing covered that shall not be revealed, nor hid which shall not be known; all will be examined in the searching, penetrating light of God's omniscience and glory, and by him whose eyes are as a flame of fire; and truth and right shall be made plainly to appear, being stripped of every veil; and all error, falsehood, unrighteousness, and injury shall be laid open, stripped of every disguise; every specious pretence, every cavil, and all false reasoning shall vanish in a moment, as not being able to bear the light of that day. And then our hearts will be turned inside out, and the secrets of them will be made more plainly to appear than our outward actions do now. Then it shall appear what the ends are which we have aimed at, what have been the governing principles which we have acted from, and what have been the dispositions we have exercised in our ecclesiastical disputes and contests. Then it will appear whether I acted uprightly, and from a truly conscientious, careful regard to my duty to my great Lord and Master, in some former ecclesiastical controversies, which have been attended with exceeding unhappy circumstances and consequences: it will appear whether there was any just cause for the resentment which was manifested on those occasions. And then our late grand controversy, concerning the qualifications necessary for admission to the privileges of members, in complete standing, in the visible church of Christ, will be examined and judged in all its parts and circumstances, and the whole set forth in a clear, certain, and perfect light. Then it will appear whether the doctrine which I have preached and published concerning this matter be Christ's own doctrine, whether he will not own it as one of the precious truths which have proceeded from his own mouth, and vindicate and honor as such before the whole universe. Then it will appear what is meant by "the man that comes without the wedding garment"; for that is the day spoken of, Matt. xxii. 13, "wherein such a one shall be bound hand and foot, and cast into outer darkness, where shall be weeping and gnashing of teeth." And then it will appear whether, in declaring this doctrine, and acting agreeable to it, and in my general conduct in the affair, I have been influenced from any regard to my own temporal interest or honor, or desire to appear wiser than others; or have acted from any sinister, secular views whatsoever; and whether what I have done has not been from a careful, strict, and tender regard to the will of my Lord and Master, and because I dare not offend him, being satisfied what his will was, after a long, diligent, impartial, and prayerful inquiry; having this constantly in view and prospect, to engage me to great solicitude not rashly to determine truth to be on this side of the question, where I am now persuaded it is, that such a determination would not be for my temporal interest, but every way against it, bringing a long series of extreme difficulties, and plunging me into an abyss of trouble and sorrow. And then it will appear whether my people have done their duty to their pastor with respect to this matter; whether they have shown a right temper and spirit on this occasion; whether they have done me justice in hearing, attending to and considering what I had to say in evidence of what I believed and taught as part of the counsel of God; whether I have been treated with that impartiality, candor, and regard which the just Judge esteemed due; and whether, in the many steps which have been taken, and the many things that have been said and done in the course of this controversy, righteousness and charity, and Christian decorum have been maintained; or, if otherwise, to how great a degree these things have been violated. Then every step of the conduct of each of us in this affair, from first to last, and the spirit we have exercised in all shall be examined and manifested, and our own consciences shall speak plain and loud, and each of us shall be convinced, and the world shall know; and never shall there be any more mistake, misrepresentation, or misapprehension of the affair to eternity.

This controversy is now probably brought to an issue between you and me as to this world; it has issued in the event of the week before last; but it must have another decision at that great day, which certainly will come, when you and I shall meet together before the great judgment seat: and therefore I leave it to that time, and shall say no more about it at present.

But I would now proceed to address myself particularly to several sorts of persons.

I. To those who are professors of godliness amongst us.

I would now call you to a serious consideration of that great day wherein you must meet him who has heretofore been your pastor, before the Judge whose eyes are as a flame of fire.

I have endeavored according to my best ability, to search the word of God, with regard to the distinguishing notes of true piety, those by which persons might best discover their state, and most surely and clearly judge of themselves. And these rules and marks I have from time to time applied to you, in the preaching of the word to the utmost of my skill, and in the most plain and search- manner that I have been able, in order to the detecting the deceived hypocrite, and establishing the hopes and comforts of the sincere. And yet it is to be feared, that after all that I have done, I now leave some of you in a deceived, deluded state; for it is not to be supposed that among several hundred professors, none are deceived.

Henceforward I am like to have no more opportunity

to take the care and charge of your souls, to examine and search them. But still I entreat you to remember and consider the rules which I have often laid down to you during my ministry, with a solemn regard to the future day when you and I must meet together before our Judge; when the uses of examination you have heard from me must be rehearsed again before you, and those rules of trial must be tried, and it will appear whether they have been good or not; and it will also appear whether you have impartially heard them, and tried yourselves by them; and the Judge himself, who is infallible, will try both you and me: and after this none will be deceived concerning the state of their souls.

I have often put you in mind, that whatever your pretences to experiences, discoveries, comforts, and joys have been, at that day every one will be judged according to his works; and then you will find it so.

May you have a minister, of greater knowledge of the word of God, and better acquaintance with soul cases, and of greater skill in applying himself to souls, whose discourses may be more searching and convincing; that such of you as have held fast deceit under my preaching, may have your eyes opened by his; that you may be undeceived before that great day.

What means and helps for instruction and self-examination you may hereafter have is uncertain; but one thing is certain, that the time is short, your opportunity for rectifying mistakes in so important a concern will soon come to an end. We live in a world of great changes. There is now a great change come to pass; a controversy is at an end which you have continued for so many years: but the time is coming, and will soon come, when you will pass out of time into eternity; and so will pass from under all means of grace whatsoever.

The greater part of you who are professors of godliness have (to use the phrase of the apostle) "acknowledged me, in part:" you have heretofore acknowledged me to be your spiritual father, the instrument of the greatest good to you that ever is, or can be obtained by any of the children of men. Consider of that day when you and I shall meet before our Judge, when it shall be examined whether you have had from me the treatment which is due to spiritual children, and whether you have treated me as you ought to have treated a spiritual father. As the relation of a natural parent brings great obligations on children in the sight of God; so much more, in many respects, does the relation of a spiritual father bring great obligations on such whose conversation and eternal salvation they suppose God has made them the instruments of: 1 Cor. iv. 15, "For though you have ten thousand instructors in Christ, yet have ye not many fathers; for in Christ Jesus, I have begotten you through the gospel."

II. Now I am taking my leave of this people I would apply myself to such among them as I leave in a Christless, graceless condition; and would call on such seriously to consider of that solemn day when they and I must meet before the Judge of the world.

My parting with you is in some respects in a peculiar manner a melancholy parting; inasmuch as I leave you in most melancholy circumstances; because I leave you in the gall of bitterness, and bond of iniquity, having the wrath of God abiding on you, and remaining under condemnation to everlasting misery and destruction. Seeing I must leave you, it would have been a comfortable and happy circumstance of our parting, if I had left you in Christ, safe and blessed in that sure refuge and glorious rest of the saints. But it is otherwise. I leave you far off, aliens and strangers, wretched subjects and captives of sin and Satan, and prisoners of vindictive justice; without Christ, and without God in the world.

Your consciences bear me witness, that while I had opportunity, I have not ceased to warn you, and set before you your danger. I have studied to represent the misery and necessity of your circumstances in the clearest manner possible. I have tried all ways that I could think of tending to awaken your consciences, and make you sensible of the necessity of your improving your time, and being speedy in flying from the wrath to come, and thorough in the use of means for your escape and safety. I have diligently endeavored to find out and use the most powerful motives to persuade you to take care for your own welfare and salvation. I have not only endeavored to awaken you, that you might be moved with fear, but I have used my utmost endeavors to win you: I have sought out acceptable words, that if possible I might prevail upon you to forsake sin, and turn to God, and accept of Christ as your Saviour and Lord. I have spent my strength very much in these things. But yet, with regard to you whom I am now speaking to, I have not been successful; but have this day reason to complain in those words, Jer. vi. 29: "The bellows are burnt, the lead is consumed of the fire, the founder melteth in vain, for the wicked are not plucked away." It is to be feared that all my labors, as to many of you, have served no other purpose but to harden you; and that the word which I have preached, instead of being a savor of life unto life, has been a savor of death unto death. Though I shall not have any account to give for the future of such as have openly and resolutely renounced my ministry, as of a betrustment committed to me: yet remember you must give account for yourselves, of your care of your own souls, and your improvement of all means past and future, through your whole lives. God only knows what will become of your poor perishing souls, what means you may hereafter enjoy, or what disadvantages and temptations you may be under. May God in his mercy grant, that however all past means have been unsuccessful, you may have future means which may have a new effect; and that the word of God, as it shall be hereafter dispensed to you, may prove as the fire and the hammer that breaketh the rock in pieces. However, let me now at parting exhort and beseech you not wholly to forget the warnings you have had while under my ministry. When you and I shall meet at the day of judgment, then you will remember them; the sight of me, your former minister, on that occasion, will soon revive them in your memory; and that in a very affecting manner. O do not let that be the first time that they are so revived!

You and I are now parting one from another as to this world; let us labor that we may not be parted after our meeting at the last day. If I have been your faithful pastor (which will that day appear whether I have or no), then I shall be acquitted, and shall ascend with Christ. O do your part, that in such a case, it may not be so, that you should be forced eternally to part from me, and all that have been faithful in Christ Jesus. This is a sorrowful parting that now is between you and me, but that would be a more sorrowful parting to you than this. This you may perhaps bear without being much affected with it, if you are not glad of it; but such a parting in that day will most deeply, sensibly, and dreadfully affect you.

III. I would address myself to those who are under some awakenings.

Blessed be God that there are some such, and that (although I have reason to fear I leave multitudes in this large congregation in a Christless state) yet I do not leave them all in total stupidity and carelessness about their souls. Some of you, that I have reason to hope are under some awakenings, have acquainted me with your circumstances; which has a tendency to cause me, now I am leaving you, to take my leave of you with peculiar concern for you. What will be the issue of your present exercise of mind I know not: but it will be known at that day, when you and I shall meet before the judgment seat of Christ. Therefore now be much in consideration of that day.

Now I am parting with this flock, I would once more press upon you the counsels I have heretofore given, to take heed of being slightly in so great a concern, to be thorough and in good earnest in the affair, and to beware of backsliding, to hold on and hold out to the end. And cry mightily to God, that these great changes that pass over this church and congregation do not prove your overthrow. There is great temptation in them; and the devil will undoubtedly seek to make his advantage of them, if possible to cause your present convictions and endeavors to be abortive. You had need to double your diligence, and watch and pray, lest you be overcome by temptation.

Whoever may hereafter stand related to you as your spiritual guide, my desire and prayer is, that the great Shepherd of the sheep would have a special respect to you, and be your guide (for there is none teacheth like him), and that he who is the infinite fountain of light, would "open your eyes, and turn you from darkness unto light, and from the power of Satan unto God; that you may receive forgiveness of sins, and inheritance among them that are sanctified, through faith that is in Christ"; that so, in that great day, when I shall meet you again before your Judge and mine, we may meet in joyful and glorious circumstances, never to be separated any more.

IV. I would apply myself to the young people of the congregation.

Since I have been settled in the work of the ministry in this place, I have ever had a peculiar concern for the souls of the young people, and a desire that religion might flourish among them: and have especially exerted myself in order to it; because I knew the special opportunity they had beyond others, and that ordinarily those whom God intended mercy for, were brought to fear and love him in their youth. And it has ever appeared to me a peculiarly amiable thing, to see young people walking in the ways of virtue and Christian piety, having their hearts purified and sweetened with a principle of divine love. And it has appeared a thing exceeding beautiful, and what would be much to the adorning and happiness of the town, if the young people could be persuaded when they meet together, to converse as Christians, and as the children of God; avoiding impurity, levity and extravagance; keeping strictly to the rules of virtue, and conversing together of the things of God, and Christ, and heaven. This is what I have longed for: and it has been exceeding grievous to me when I have heard of vice, vanity and disorder among our youth. And so far as I know my own heart, it was from hence that I formerly led this church to some measures, for the suppressing vice among our young people, which gave so great offence, and by which I became so obnoxious. I have sought the good, and not the hurt of our young people. I have desired their truest honor and happiness, and not their reproach; knowing that true virtue and religion tended not only to the glory and felicity of young people in another world, but their greatest peace and prosperity, and highest dignity and honor in this world; and above all things to sweeten, and render pleasant and delightful, even the days of youth.

But whether I have loved you, and sought your good more or less, yet God in his providence, now calling me to part with you, committing your souls to him who once committed the pastoral care of them to me, nothing remains, but only (as I am now taking my leave of you) earnestly to beseech you, from love to yourselves, if you have none to me, not to despise and forget the warnings and counsels I have so often given you; remembering the day when you and I must meet again before the great

Judge of quick and dead; when it will appear whether the things I have taught you were true, whether the counsels I have given you were good, and whether I truly sought your good, and whether you have well improved my endeavors.

I have, from time to time, earnestly warned you agains frolicking (as it is called), and some other liberties commonly taken by young people in the land. And whatever some may say in justification of such liberties and customs, and may laugh at warnings against them, I now leave you my parting testimony against such things; not doubting but God will approve and confirm it in that day when we shall meet before him.

V. I would apply myself to the children of the congregation, the lambs of this flock, who have been so long under my care.

I have just now said that I have had a peculiar concern for the young people; and in so saying I did not intend to exclude you. You are in youth, and in the most early youth: and therefore I have been sensible that if those that were young had a precious opportunity for their souls' good, you who are very young had, in many respects, a peculiarly precious opportunity. And accordingly I have not neglected you: I have endeavored to do the part of a faithful shepherd, in feeding the lambs as well as the sheep. Christ did once commit the care of your souls to me as your minister; and you know, dear children, how I have instructed you, and warned you from time to time; you know how I have often called you together for that end; and some of you, sometimes, have seemed to be affected with what I have said to you. But I am afraid it has had no saving effects as to many of you; but that you remain still in an unconverted condition, without any real saving work wrought in your souls, convincing you thoroughly of your sin and misery, causing you to see the great evil of sin, and to mourn for it, and hate it above all things, and giving you a sense of the excellency of the Lord Jesus Christ, bringing you with all your hearts to cleave to him as your Saviour, weaning your hearts from the world, and causing you to love God above all, and to delight in holiness more than in all the pleasant things of this earth; and so that I now leave you in a miserable condition, having no interest in Christ, and so under the awful displeasure and anger of God, and in danger of going down to the pit of eternal misery.

But now I must bid you farewell: I must leave you in the hands of God; I can do no more for you than to pray for you. Only I desire you not to forget, but often think of the counsels and warnings I have given you, and the endeavors I have used, that your souls might be saved from everlasting destruction.

Dear children, I leave you in an evil world, that is full of snares and temptations. God only knows what will become of you. This the Scripture hath told us, that there are but few saved; and we have abundant confirmation of it from what we see. This we see, that children die as well as others; multitudes die before they grow up; and of those that grow up, comparatively few ever give good evidence of saving conversion to God. I pray God to pity you, and take care of you, and provide for you the best means for the good of your souls; and that God himself would undertake for you to be your heavenly Father, and the mighty Redeemer of your immortal souls. Do not neglect to pray for yourselves: take heed you be not of the number of those who cast off fear, and restrain prayer before God. Constantly pray to God in secret; and often remember that great day when you must appear before the judgment seat of Christ, and meet your minister there, who has so often counselled and warned you.

I conclude with a few words of advice to all in general, in some particulars, which are of great importance in order to the welfare and prosperity of this church and congregation.

1. One thing that greatly concerns you, as you would be a happy people, is the maintaining of *family order*.

We have had great disputes how the church ought to be regulated; and indeed the subject of these disputes was of great importance: but the due regulation of your families is of no less, and, in some respects, of much greater importance. Every Christian family ought to be as it were a little church, consecrated to Christ, and wholly influenced and governed by his rules. And family education and order are some of the chief of the means of grace. If these fail, all other means are like to prove ineffectual. If these are daily maintained, all the means of grace will be like to prosper and be successful.

Let me now, therefore, once more, before I finally cease to speak to this congregation, repeat and earnestly press the counsel which I have often urged on heads of families here, while I was their pastor, to great painfulness, in teaching, warning, and directing their children; bringing them up in the nurture and admonition of the Lord; beginning early, when there is yet opportunity, and maintaining a constant diligence in labors of this kind; remembering that, as you would not have all your instructions and counsels ineffectual, there must be government as well as instructions, which must be maintained with an even hand, and steady resolution, as a guard to the religion and morals of the family, and the support of its good order. Take heed that it be not with any of you as with Eli of old, who reproved his children but restrained them not; and that, by this means, you do not bring the like curse on your families as he did on his.

And let children obey their parents, and yield to their instructions, and submit to their orders, as they would inherit a blessing and not a curse. For we have reason to think, from many things in the word of God, that nothing has a greater tendency to bring a curse on persons in this world, and on all their temporal concerns, than an undutiful, unsubmissive, disorderly behavior in children towards their parents.

2. As you would seek the future prosperity of this society, it is of vast importance that you should avoid contention.

A contentious people will be a miserable people. The contentions which have been among you, since I first became your pastor, have been one of the greatest burdens I have labored under in the course of my ministry: not only the contentions you have had with me, but those which you have had one with another, about your lands and other concerns. Because I knew that contention, heat of spirit, evil speaking, and things of the like nature, were directly contrary to the spirit of Christianity, and did, in a peculiar manner, tend to drive away God's Spirit from a people, and to render all means of grace ineffectual, as well as to destroy a people's outward comfort and welfare.

Let me therefore earnestly exhort you, as you would seek your own future good hereafter, to watch against a contentious spirit. "If you would see good days, seek peace, and ensue it," 1 Pet. iii. 10, 11. Let the contention, which has lately been about the terms of Christian communion, as it has been the greatest of your contentions, so be the last of them. I would, now I am preaching my farewell sermon, say to you, as the Apostle to the Corinthians, 2 Cor. xiii. 11, 12: "Finally, brethren, farewell. Be perfect: be of one mind: live in peace; and the God of love and peace shall be with you."

And here I would particularly advise those that have adhered to me in the late controversy, to watch over their spirits, and avoid all bitterness towards others. Your temptations are, in some respects, the greatest; because what has been lately done is grievous to you. But however wrong you may think others have done, maintain, with great diligence and watchfulness, a Christian meekness and sedateness of spirit; and labor, in this respect, to excel others who are of the contrary part. And this will be the best victory: for "he that rules his spirit, is better than he that takes a city." Therefore let nothing be done through strife or vain-glory. Indulge no revengeful spirit in any wise; but watch and pray against it; and, by all means in your power, seek the prosperity of the town: and never think you behave yourselves as becomes Christians, but when you sincerely, sensibly, and fervently love all men, of whatever party or opinion, and whether friendly or unkind, just or injurious, to you or your friends, or to the cause and kingdom of Christ.

3. Another thing that vastly concerns the future prosperity of this town, is, that you should watch against the encroachments of error; and particularly Arminianism, and doctrines of like tendency.

You were, many of you, as I well remember, much alarmed with the apprehension of the danger of the prevailing of these corrupt principles, near sixteen years ago. But the danger then was small in comparison of what appears now. These doctrines at this day are much more prevalent than they were then: the progress they have made in the land, within this seven years, seems to have been vastly greater than at any time in the like space before: and they are still prevailing and creeping into almost all parts of the land, threatening the utter ruin of the credit of those doctrines which are the peculiar glory of the gospel, and the interests of vital piety. And I have of late perceived some things among yourselves, that show that you are far from being out of danger, but on the contrary remarkably exposed. The older people may perhaps think themselves sufficiently fortified against infection; but it is fit that all should beware of self-confidence and carnal security, and should remember those needful warnings of sacred writ, "Be not high-minded, but fear; and let him that stands, take heed lest he fall." But let the case of the older people be as it will, the rising generation are doubtless greatly exposed. These principles are exceeding taking with corrupt nature, and are what young people, at least such as have not their hearts established with grace, are easily led away with.

And if these principles should greatly prevail in this town, as they very lately have done in another large town I could name, formerly greatly noted for religion, and so for a long time, it will threaten the spiritual and eternal ruin of this people, in the present and future generations. Therefore you have need of the greatest and most diligent care and watchfulness with respect to this matter.

4. Another thing which I would advise to, that you may hereafter be a prosperous people, is, that you would give yourselves much to prayer.

God is the fountain of all blessing and prosperity, and he will be sought to for his blessing. I would therefore advise you not only to be constant in secret and family prayer, and in the public worship of God in his house, but also often to assemble yourselves in private praying societies. I would advise all such as are grieved for the afflictions of Joseph, and sensibly affected with the calamities of this town, of whatever opinion they be with relation to the subject of our late controversy, often to meet together for prayer, and to cry to God for his mercy to themselves, and mercy to this town, and mercy to Zion and the people of God in general through the world.

5. The last article of advice I would give (which doubtless does greatly concern your prosperity), is, that you would take great care with regard to the settlement of a minister, to see to it who, or what manner of person he is that you settle; and particularly in these two respects,

(1.) That he be a man of thoroughly sound principles in the scheme of doctrine which he maintains.

This you will stand in the greatest need of, especially

at such a day of corruption as this is. And in order to obtain such a one, you had need to exercise extraordinary care and prudence. I know the danger. I know the manner of many young gentlemen of corrupt principles, their ways of concealing themselves, the fair specious disguises they are wont to put on, by which they deceive others, to maintain their own credit, and get themselves into others' confidence and improvement, and secure and establish their own interest, until they see a convenient opportunity to begin more openly to broach and propagate their corrupt tenets.

(2.) Labor to obtain a man who has an established character, as a person of serious religion and fervent piety.

It is of vast importance that those who are settled in this work should be men of true piety, at all times, and in all places; but more especially at some times, and in some towns and churches. And this present time, which is a time wherein religion is in danger, by so many corruptions in doctrine and practice, is in a peculiar manner a day wherein such ministers are necessary. Nothing else but sincere piety of heart is at all to be depended on, at such a time as this, as a security to a young man, just coming into the world, from the prevailing infection, or thoroughly to engage him in proper and successful endeavors to withstand and oppose the torrent of error, and prejudice, against the high, mysterious, evangelical doctrines of the religion of Jesus Christ, and their genuine effects in true experimental religion. And this place is a place that does peculiarly need such a minister, for reasons obvious to all.

If you should happen to settle a minister who knows nothing truly of Christ, and the way of salvation by him, nothing experimentally of the nature of vital religion; alas, how will you be exposed as sheep without a shepherd! Here is need of one in this place, who shall be eminently fit to stand in the gap, and make up the hedge, and who shall be as the chariots of Israel, and the horsemen thereof. You need one that shall stand as a champion in the cause of truth and the power of godliness.

Having briefly mentioned these important articles of advice, nothing remains, but that I now take my leave of you, and bid you all *farewell*; wishing and praying for your best prosperity. I would now commend your immortal souls to Him, who formerly committed them to me, expecting the day, when I must meet you again before Him, who is the Judge of quick and dead. I desire that I may never forget this people, who have been so long my special charge, and that I may never cease fervently to pray for your prosperity. May God bless you with a faithful pastor, one that is well acquainted with his mind and will, thoroughly warning sinners, wisely and skilfully searching professors, and conducting you in the way to eternal blessedness. May you have truly a burning and shining light set up in this candlestick; and may you, not only for a season, but during his whole life, and that a long life, be willing to rejoice in his light.

And let me be remembered in the prayers of all God's people that are of a calm spirit, and are peaceable and faithful in Israel, of whatever opinion they may be with respect to terms of church communion.

And let us all remember, and never forget our future solemn meeting on that great day of the Lord; the day of infallible decision, and of the everlasting and unalterable sentence. AMEN.

RELIGIOUS AFFECTIONS

1 PETER i. 8.—Whom having not seen, ye love; in whom, though now ye see him not, yet believing, ye rejoice with joy unspeakable, and full of glory.

In these words, the apostle represents the state of the minds of the Christians he wrote to, under the persecutions they were then the subjects of. These persecutions are what he has respect to, in the two preceding verses, when he speaks of *the trial of their faith*, and of *their being in heaviness through manifold temptations*.

Such trials are of threefold benefit to true religion. Hereby the truth of it is manifested, and it appears to be indeed true religion; they, above all other things, have a tendency to distinguish between true religion and false, and to cause the difference between them evidently to appear. Hence they are called by the name of *trials*, in the verse nextly preceding the text, and in innumerable other places; they try the faith and religion of professors, of what sort it is, as apparent gold is tried in the fire, and manifested, whether it be true gold or no. And the faith of true Christians being thus tried and proved to be true, is "found to praise, and honor, and glory," as in that preceding verse.

And then, these trials are of further benefit to true religion; they not only manifest the truth of it, but they make its genuine beauty and amiableness remarkably to appear. True virtue never appears so lovely, as when it is most oppressed; and the divine excellency of real Christianity, is never exhibited with such advantage, as when under the greatest trials: then it is that true faith appears much more precious than gold! And upon this account is "found to praise, and honor, and glory."

And again, another benefit that such trials are of to true religion, is, that they purify and increase it. They not only manifest it to be true, but also tend to refine it, and deliver it from those mixtures of that which is false, which encumber and impede it; that nothing may be left but that which is true. They tend to cause the amiableness of true religion to appear to the best advantage, as was before observed; and not only so, but they tend to increase its beauty, by establishing and confirming it, and making it more lively and vigorous, and purifying it from those things that obscured its lustre and glory. As gold that is tried in the fire, is purged from its alloy, and all remainders of dross, and comes forth more solid and beautiful; so true faith being tried as gold is tried in the fire, becomes more precious, and thus also is "found unto praise, and honor, and glory." The apostle seems to have respect to each of these benefits, that persecutions are of to true religion, in the verse preceding the text.

And in the text, the apostle observes how true religion operated in the Christians he wrote to, under their persecutions, whereby these benefits of persecution appeared in them; or what manner of operation of true religion, in them, it was, whereby their religion, under persecution, was manifested to be true religion, and also appeared to be increased and purified, and so was like to be "found unto praise, and honor, and glory, at the appearing of Jesus Christ." And there were two kinds of operation, or exercise of true religion, in them, under their sufferings, that the apostle takes notice of in the text, wherein these benefits appeared.

1. *Love to Christ*: "Whom having not yet seen, ye love." The world was ready to wonder, what strange principle it was, that influenced them to expose them-

selves to so great sufferings, to forsake the things that were seen, and renounce all that was dear and pleasant, which was the object of sense. They seemed to the men of the world about them, as though they were beside themselves, and to act as though they hated themselves; there was nothing in their view, that could induce them thus to suffer, and support them under, and carry them through such trials. But although there was nothing that was seen, nothing that the world saw, or that the Christians themselves ever saw with their bodily eyes, that thus influenced and supported them, yet they had a supernatural principle of love to something unseen; they loved Jesus Christ, for they saw him spiritually whom the world saw not, and whom they themselves had never seen with bodily eyes.

2. *Joy in Christ.* Though their outward sufferings were very grievous, yet their inward spiritual joys were greater than their sufferings; and these supported them, and enabled them to suffer with cheerfulness.

There are two things which the apostle takes notice of in the text concerning this joy. 1. The manner in which it rises, the way in which Christ, though unseen, is the foundation of it, viz., by faith; which is the evidence of things not seen: "In whom, though now ye see him not, yet believing, ye rejoice." 2. The nature of the joy; "unspeakable and full of glory." Unspeakable in the kind of it; very different from worldly joys, and carnal delights; of a vastly more pure, sublime, and heavenly nature, being something supernatural, and truly divine, and so ineffably excellent; the sublimity and exquisite sweetness of which, there were no words to set forth. Unspeakable also in degree; it pleasing God to give them this holy joy, with a liberal hand, and in large measure, in their state of persecution.

Their joy was full of glory. Although the joy was unspeakable, and no words were sufficient to describe it, yet something might be said of it, and no words more fit to represent its excellency than these, that it was *full of glory*; or, as it is in the original, *glorified joy*. In rejoicing with this joy, their minds were filled, as it were, with a glorious brightness, and their natures exalted and perfected. It was a most worthy, noble rejoicing, that did not corrupt and debase the mind, as many carnal joys do; but did greatly beautify and dignify it; it was a prelibation of the joy of heaven, that raised their minds to a degree of heavenly blessedness; it filled their minds with a light of God's glory, and made themselves to shine with some communication of that glory.

Hence the proposition or doctrine, that I would raise from these words, is this:

DOCTRINE. *True religion, in great part, consists in holy affections.*

We see that the apostle, in observing and remarking the operations and exercises of religion in the Christians he wrote to, wherein their religion appeared to be true and of the right kind, when it had its greatest trial of what sort it was, being tried by persecution as gold is tried in the fire, and when their religion not only proved true, but was most pure, and cleansed from its dross and mixtures of that which was not true, and when religion appeared in them most in its genuine excellency and native beauty, and was found to praise, and honor, and glory; he singles out the religious affections of *love* and *joy*, that were then in exercise in them: these are the exercises of religion he takes notice of, wherein their religion did thus appear true and pure, and in its proper glory. Here I would,

1. Show what is intended by the affections.

2. Observe some things which make it evident, that a great part of the religion lies in the affections.

I. It may be inquired, what the affections of the mind are?

I answer: The affections are no other than the more vigorous and sensible exercises of the inclination and will of the soul.

God has indued the soul with two faculties: one is that by which it is capable of perception and speculation, or by which it discerns, and views, and judges of things; which is called the understanding. The other faculty is that by which the soul does not merely perceive and view things, but is some way inclined with respect to the things it views or considers; either is inclined *to* them, or is disinclined and averse *from* them; or is the faculty by which the soul does not behold things, as an indifferent unaffected spectator, but either as liking or disliking, pleased or displeased, approving or rejecting. This faculty is called by various names; it is sometimes called the *inclination*: and, as it has respect to the actions that are determined and governed by it, is called the *will*: and the mind, with regard to the exercises of this faculty, is often called the *heart*.

The exercises of this faculty are of two sorts; either those by which the soul is carried out towards the things that are in view, in approving of them, being pleased with them, and inclined to them; or those in which the soul opposes the things that are in view, in disapproving of them, and in being displeased with them, averse from them, and rejecting them.

And as the exercises of the inclination and will of the soul are various in their kinds, so they are much more various in their degrees. There are some exercises of pleasedness or displeasedness, inclination or disinclination, wherein the soul is carried but a little beyond a state of perfect indifference.—And there are other degrees above this, wherein the approbation or dislike, pleasedness or aversion, are stronger, wherein we may rise higher and higher, till the soul comes to act vigorously and sensibly, and the actings of the soul are with that **strength, that (through the laws of the union which the**

Creator has fixed between the soul and the body) the motion of the blood and animal spirits begins to be sensibly altered; whence oftentimes arises some bodily sensation, especially about the heart and vitals, that are the fountain of the fluids of the body: from whence it comes to pass, that the mind, with regard to the exercises of this faculty, perhaps in all nations and ages, is called the *heart*. And, it is to be noted, that they are these more vigorous and sensible exercises of this faculty that are called the *affections*.

The will, and the affections of the soul, are not two faculties; the affections are not essentially distinct from the will, nor do they differ from the mere actings of the will, and inclination of the soul, but only in the liveliness and sensibleness of exercise.

It must be confessed, that language is here somewhat imperfect, and the meaning of words in a considerable measure loose and unfixed, and not precisely limited by custom, which governs the use of language. In some sense, the affection of the soul differs nothing at all from the will and inclination, and the will never is in any exercise any further than it is affected; it is not moved out of a state of perfect indifference, any otherwise than as it is affected one way or other, and acts nothing any further. But yet there are many actings of the will and inclination, that are not so commonly called *affections*: in every thing we do, wherein we act voluntarily, there is an exercise of the will and inclination; it is our inclination that governs us in our actions; but all the actings of the inclination and will, in all our common actions of life, are not ordinarily called affections. Yet, what are commonly called affections are not essentially different from them, but only in the degree and manner of exercise. In every act of the will whatsoever, the soul either likes or dislikes, is either inclined or disinclined to what is in view: these are not essentially different from those affections of love and hatred: that liking or inclination of the soul to a thing, if it be in a high degree, and be vigorous and lively, is the very same thing with the affection of love; and that disliking and disinclining, if in a greater degree, is the very same with hatred. In every act of the will for, or towards something not present, the soul is in some degree inclined to that thing; and that inclination, if in a considerable degree, is the very same with the affection of desire. And in every degree of the act of the will, wherein the soul approves of something present, there is a degree of pleasedness; and that pleasedness, if it be in a considerable degree, is the very same with the affections of joy or delight. And if the will disapproves of what is present, the soul is in some degree displeased, and if that displeasedness be great, it is the very same with the affection of grief or sorrow.

Such seems to be our nature, and such the laws of the union of soul and body, that there never is in any case whatsoever, any lively and vigorous exercise of the will or inclination of the soul, without some effect upon the body, in some alteration of the motion of its fluids, and especially of the animal spirits. And, on the other hand, from the same laws of the union of the soul and body, the constitution of the body, and the motion of its fluids, may promote the exercise of the affections. But yet it is not the body, but the mind only, that is the proper seat of the affections. The body of man is no more capable of being really the subject of love or hatred, joy or sorrow, fear or hope, than the body of a tree, or than the same body of man is capable of thinking and understanding. As it is the soul only that has ideas, so it is the soul only that is pleased or displeased with its ideas. As it is the soul only that thinks, so it is the soul only that loves or hates, rejoices or is grieved at what it thinks of. Nor are these motions of the animal spirits, and fluids of the body, any thing properly belonging to the nature of the affections, though they always accompany them, in the present state; but are only effects or concomitants of the affections that are entirely distinct from the affections themselves, and no way essential to them; so that an unbodied spirit may be as capable of love and hatred, joy or sorrow, hope or fear, or other affections, as one that is united to a body.

The affections and passions are frequently spoken of as the same; and yet in the more common use of speech, there is in some respect a difference; and affection is a word that in its ordinary signification, seems to be something more extensive than passion, being used for all vigorous lively actings of the will or inclination; but passion for those that are more sudden, and whose effects on the animal spirits are more violent, and the mind more overpowered, and less in its own command.

As all the exercises of the inclination and will, are either in approving and liking, or disapproving and rejecting; so the affections are of two sorts; they are those by which the soul is carried out to what is in view, cleaving to it, or seeking it; or those by which it is averse from it, and opposes it.

Of the former sort are love, desire, hope, joy, gratitude, complacence. Of the latter kind are hatred, fear, anger, grief, and such like; which it is needless now to stand particularly to define.

And there are some affections wherein there is a composition of each of the aforementioned kinds of actings of the will; as in the affection of *pity*, there is something of the former kind, towards the person suffering, and something of the latter towards what he suffers. And so in zeal, there is in it high approbation of some person or thing, together with vigorous opposition to what is conceived to be contrary to it.

There are other mixed affections that might be also mentioned, but I hasten to,

II. The second thing proposed, which was to observe some things that render it evident, that true religion, in great part consists in the affections. . . .

The Scriptures do represent true religion, as being summarily comprehended in love, the chief of the affections, and fountain of all other affections.

So our blessed Saviour represents the matter, in answer to the lawyer, who asked him, which was the great commandment of the law Matt. xxii. 37–40: "Jesus said unto him, Thou shalt love the Lord thy God with all thy heart, and with all thy soul, and with all thy mind. This is the first and great commandment. And the second is like unto it, Thou shalt love thy neighbor as thyself. On these two commandments hang all the law and the prophets." And the apostle Paul does from time to time make the same representation of the matter; as in Rom. xiii. 8, "He that loveth another, hath fulfilled the law." And ver. 10, "Love is the fulfilling of the law." And Gal. v. 14, "For all the law is fulfilled in one word, even in this, Thou shalt love thy neighbor as thyself." So likewise in 1 Tim. i. 5, "Now the end of the commandment is charity, out of a pure heart," &c. So the same apostle speaks of love, as the greatest thing in religion, and as the vitals, essence and soul of it; without which, the greatest knowledge and gifts, and the most glaring profession, and every thing else which appertains to religion, are vain and worthless; and represents it as the fountain from whence proceeds all that is good, in 1 Cor. xiii. throughout; for that which is there rendered *charity*, in the original is [*agape*], the proper English of which is *love*.

Now, although it be true, that the love thus spoken of includes the whole of a sincerely benevolent propensity of the soul towards God and man; yet it may be considered, that it is evident from what has been before observed, that this propensity or inclination of the soul, when in sensible and vigorous exercise, becomes affection, and is no other than affectionate love. And surely it is such vigorous and fervent love which Christ speaks of, as the sum of all religion, when he speaks of loving God with all our hearts, with all our souls, and with all our minds, and our neighbor as ourselves, as the sum of all that was taught and prescribed in the law and the prophets.

Indeed it cannot be supposed, when this affection of love is here, and in other Scriptures, spoken of as the sum of all religion, that hereby is meant the act, exclusive of the habit, or that the exercise of the understanding is excluded, which is implied in all reasonable affection. But it is doubtless true, and evident from these Scriptures, that the essence of all true religion lies in holy love; and that in this divine affection, and an habitual disposition to it, and that light which is the foundation of it, and those things which are the fruits of it, consists the whole of religion.

From hence it clearly and certainly appears, that great part of true religion consists in the affections. For love is not only one of the affections, but it is the first and chief of the affections, and the fountain of all the affections. From love arises hatred of those things which are contrary to what we love, or which oppose and thwart us in those things that we delight in: and from the various exercises of love and hatred, according to the circumstances of the objects of these affections, as present or absent, certain or uncertain, probable or improbable, arise all those other affections of desire, hope, fear, joy, grief, gratitude, anger, &c. From a vigorous, affectionate, and fervent love to God, will necessarily arise other religious affections; hence will arise an intense hatred and abhorrence of sin, fear of sin, and a dread of God's displeasure, gratitude to God for his goodness, complacence and joy in God, when God is graciously and sensibly present, and grief when he is absent, and a joyful hope when a future enjoyment of God is expected, and fervent zeal for the glory of God. And in like manner, from a fervent love to men, will arise all other virtuous affections towards men.

FREEDOM OF THE WILL

Conclusion

Whether the things which have been alleged, are liable to any tolerable answer in the way of calm, intelligible and strict reasoning, I must leave others to judge; but I am sensible they are liable to one sort of answer. It is not unlikely that some, who value themselves on the supposed rational and generous principles of the modern, fashionable divinity, will have their indignation and disdain raised at the sight of this discourse, and on perceiving what things are pretended to be proved in it. And if they think it worthy of being read, or of so much notice as to say much about it, they may probably renew the usual exclamations, with additional vehemence and contempt, about the *fate of the heathen*, Hobbes' *necessity*, and *making men mere machines*; accumulating the terrible epithets of *fatal, unfrustrable, inevitable, irresistible*, &c., and it may be, with the addition of *horrid* and *blasphemous*; and perhaps much skill may be used to set forth things, which have been said, in colors which shall be shocking to the imaginations, and moving to the passions of those, who have either too little capacity, or too much confidence of the opinions they have imbibed, and contempt of the contrary, to try the matter by any serious and circumspect examination. Or difficulties may be started and insisted on, which do not belong to the controversy; because, let them be more or less real, and hard to be resolved, they are not what are owing to any thing distinguishing of this scheme from that of the Arminians, and would not be removed nor diminished by renouncing the former, and adhering to the latter. Or some particular things may be picked out, which they may think will sound harshest in the ears of the generality; and these may be glossed and descanted on, with tart and contemptuous words; and from thence, the whole treated with triumph and insult.

It is easy to see, how the decision of most of the points in controversy, between *Calvinists* and *Arminians*, depends on the determination of this grand article concerning the *freedom of the Will, requisite to moral agency*; and that by clearing and establishing the *Calvinistic* doctrine in this point, the chief arguments are obviated, by which *Arminian* doctrines in general are supported, and the contrary doctrines demonstratively confirmed. Hereby it becomes manifest, that God's moral government over mankind, his treating them as moral agents, making them the objects of his commands, counsels, calls, warnings, expostulations, promises, threatenings, rewards and punishments, is not inconsistent with a *determining disposal* of all events, of every kind, throughout the universe, in his *Providence*; either by positive efficiency, or permission. Indeed, such an *universal, determining Providence* infers some kind of necessity of all events, such a necessity as implies an infallible, previous fixedness of the futurity of the event; but no other necessity of moral events, or volitions of intelligent agents, is needful in order to this, than *moral necessity*; which does as much ascertain the futurity of the event, as any other necessity. But, as has been demonstrated, such a necessity is not at all repugnant to moral agency, and a reasonable use of commands, calls, rewards, punishments, &c. Yea, not only are objections of this kind against the doctrine of an universal *determining Providence*, removed by what has been said, but the truth of such a doctrine is demonstrated.

As it has been demonstrated, that the futurity of all future events is established by previous necessity, either natural or moral; so it is manifest that the Sovereign Creator and Disposer of the world has ordered this necessity, by ordering his own conduct, either in designedly acting or forbearing to act. For, as the being of the world is from God, so the circumstances in which it had its being at first, both negative and positive, must be ordered by him, in one of these ways; and all the necessary consequences of these circumstances, must be ordered by him. And God's active and positive interpositions, after the world was created, and the consequence of these interpositions; also every instance of his forbearing to interpose, and the sure consequences of this forbearance, must all be determined according to his pleasure. And therefore every event, which is the consequence of any thing whatsoever, or that is connected with any foregoing thing or circumstance, either positive or negative, as the ground or reason of its existence, must be ordered of God; either by a designed efficiency and interposition, or a designed forbearing to operate or interpose. But, as has been proved, all events whatsoever are necessarily connected with something foregoing, either positive or negative, which is the ground of their existence: it follows, therefore, that the whole series of events is thus connected with something in the state of things, either positive or negative, which is original in the series; i.e. something which is connected with nothing preceding that, but God's own immediate conduct, either his acting or forbearing to act. From whence it follows, that as God designedly orders his own conduct, and its connected consequences, it must necessarily be, that he designedly orders all things.

The things which have been said, obviate some of the chief objections of Arminians against the Calvinistic doctrine of the *total depravity and corruption of man's nature*, whereby his heart is wholly under the power of sin, and he is utterly unable, without the interposition of sovereign grace, savingly to love God, believe in Christ, or do anything that is truly good and acceptable in God's sight. For the main objection against this doctrine is, that it is inconsistent with the freedom of man's Will, consisting in indifference and self-determining power; because it supposes man to be under a necessity of sinning, and that God requires things of him in order to his avoiding eternal damnation, which he is unable to do; and that this doctrine is wholly inconsistent with the sincerity of counsels, invitations, &c. Now, this doctrine supposes *no other necessity* of sinning, than a moral necessity; which, as has been shown, does not at all excuse sin; and supposes *no other inability* to obey any command, or perform any duty, even the most spiritual and exalted, but a moral inability, which, as has been proved, does not excuse persons in the nonperformance of any good thing, or make them not to be the proper objects of commands, counsels and invitations. And moreover, it has been shown that there is not, and never can be, either in existence, or so much as in idea, any such freedom of Will, consisting in indifference and self-determination, for the sake of which this doctrine of original sin is cast out and that no such freedom is necessary, in order to the nature of sin, and a just desert of punishment.

The things which have been observed, do also take off the main objections of Arminians against the doctrine of *efficacious grace*; and at the same time prove the grace of God in a sinner's conversion (if there be any grace or divine influence in the affair) to be *efficacious*, yea, and *irresistible* too, if by irresistible is meant that which is attended with a moral necessity, which it is impossible should ever be violated by any resistance. The main objection of Arminians against this doctrine is, that it is

inconsistent with their self-determining freedom of Will;
and that it is repugnant to the nature of virtue, that it
should be wrought in the heart by the determining efficacy and power of another, instead of its being owing
to a self-moving power; that in that case, the good which
is wrought, would not be *our* virtue, but rather God's
virtue; because it is not the person in whom it is wrought,
that is the determining author of it, but God that wrought
it in him. But the things, which are the foundation of
these objections, have been considered; and it has been
demonstrated that the liberty of moral agents does not
consist in self-determining power, and that there is no
need of any such liberty in order to the nature of virtue,
nor does it at all hinder but that the state or act of the
Will may be the virtue of the subject, though it be not
from self-determination, but the determination of an
extrinsic cause; even so as to cause the event to be
morally necessary to the subject of it. And as it has been
proved, that nothing in the state or acts of the Will of
man is contingent; but that, on the contrary, every event
of this kind is necessary, by a moral necessity; and as it
has also been now demonstrated, that the doctrine of an
universal determining Providence, follows from that doctrine of necessity which was proved before; and so that
God does decisively, in his Providence, order all the
volitions of moral agents, either by positive influence or
permission; and it being allowed, on all hands, that what
God does in the affair of man's virtuous volitions, whether
it be more or less, is by some positive influence, and not
be mere permission, as in the affair of a sinful volition; if
we put these things together, it will follow, that God's
assistance or influence, must be determining and decisive,
or must be attended with a moral necessity of the event;
and so, that God gives virtue, holiness and conversion to
sinners, by an influence which determines the effect, in
such a manner, that the effect will infallibly follow by a

moral necessity; which is what Calvinists mean by efficacious and irresistible grace.

The things which have been said, do likewise answer the chief objections against the doctrine of God's *universal* and *absolute decree*, and afford infallible proof of this doctrine; and of the doctrine of *absolute, eternal, personal election* in particular. The main objections against these doctrines are, that they infer a necessity of the volitions of moral agents, and of the future, moral state and acts of men, and so are not consistent with those eternal rewards and punishments, which are connected with conversion and impenitence; nor can be made to agree with the reasonableness and sincerity of the precepts, calls, counsels, warnings and expostulations of the word of God; or with the various methods and means of grace, which God uses with sinners, to bring them to repentance; and the whole of that moral government, which God exercises towards mankind; and that they infer an inconsistence between the *secret* and *revealed* Will of God, and make God the author of sin. But all these things have been obviated in the preceding discourse. And the certain truth of these doctrines, concerning God's eternal purposes, will follow from what was just now observed concerning God's universal Providence; how it infallibly follows from what has been proved, that God orders all events; and the volitions of moral agents amongst others by such a decisive disposal, that the events are infallibly connected with his disposal. For if God disposes all events, so that the infallible existence of the events is decided by his Providence, then he, doubtless, thus orders and decides things *knowingly* and on *design*. God does not do what he does, nor order what he orders, accidentally or unawares; either *without* or *beside* his intention. And if there be a foregoing *design*, of doing and ordering as he does, this is the same with a *purpose* or *decree*. And as it has been shown that nothing is new to

God in any respect, but all things are perfectly and equally in his view from eternity; hence it will follow, that his designs or purposes are not things formed anew, founded on any new views or appearances, but are all eternal purposes. And as it has been now shown, how the doctrine of determining, efficacious grace certainly follows from things proved in the foregoing discourse; hence will necessarily follow the doctrine of *particular, eternal, absolute election.* For if men are made true saints, no otherwise than as God makes them so, and distinguishes them from others, by an efficacious power and influence of his, that decides and fixes the event; and God thus makes some saints, and not others, on design or purpose, and (as has been now observed) no designs of God are new; it follows, that God thus distinguished from others, all that ever become true saints, by his eternal design or decree. I might also show how God's certain foreknowledge must suppose an absolute decree, and how such a decree can be proved to a demonstration from it; but, that this discourse may not be lengthened out too much, that must be omitted for the present.

From these things it will inevitably follow, that however Christ in some sense may be said to *die for all,* and to redeem all visible Christians, yea, the whole world by his death; yet there must be something *particular* in the design of his death, with respect to such as he intended should actually be saved thereby. As appears by what has been now shown, God has the actual salvation or redemption of a certain number in his proper, absolute design, and of a certain number only; and therefore such a design only can be prosecuted in any thing God does, in order to the salvation of men. God pursues a proper design of the salvation of the elect in giving Christ to die, and prosecutes such a design with respect to no other, most strictly speaking: for it is impossible that God should prosecute any other design than only such as he has; he certainly does not, in the highest propriety and strictness of speech, pursue a design that he has not. And, indeed, such a particularity and limitation of redemption will as infallibly follow, from the doctrine of God's fore-knowledge, as from that of the decree. For it is as impossible, in strictness of speech, that God should prosecute a design, or aim at a thing, which He at the same time most perfectly knows will not be accomplished, as that he should use endeavors for that which is beside his decree.

By the things which have been proved, are obviated some of the main objections against the doctrine of the infallible and necessary *perseverance* of saints, and some of the main foundations of this doctrine are established. The main prejudices of Arminians against this doctrine seem to be these. They suppose such a necessary, infallible perseverance to be repugnant to the freedom of the Will; that it must be owing to man's own self-determining power, that he *first becomes* virtuous and holy; and so, in like manner, it must be left a thing contingent, to be determined by the same freedom of Will, whether he will *persevere* in virtue and holiness; and that otherwise his continuing steadfast in faith and obedience would not be his virtue, or at all praiseworthy and rewardable, nor could his perseverance be properly the matter of divine commands, counsels and promises, nor his apostasy be properly threatened, and men warned against it. Whereas we find all these things in Scripture: there we find steadfastness and perseverance in true Christianity, represented as the virtue of the saints, spoken of as praiseworthy in them, and glorious rewards promised to it; and also find that God makes it the subject of his commands, counsels and promises; and the contrary, of threatenings and warnings. But the foundation of these objections has been removed, in its being shown that moral necessity and infallible certainty of events is not inconsistent with these things; and that as to freedom of Will, lying in the power of the Will to determine itself, there neither is any such thing, nor any need of it, in order to virtue, reward, commands, counsels, &c.

And as the doctrines of efficacious grace and absolute election do certainly follow from things which have been proved in the preceding discourse; so some of the main foundations of the doctrine of perseverance, are thereby established. If the beginning of true faith and holiness, and a man's becoming a true saint at first, does not depend on the self-determining power of the Will, but on the determining, efficacious grace of God; it may well be argued, that it is so also with respect to men's being continued saints, or persevering in faith and holiness. The conversion of a sinner being not owing to a man's self-determination, but to God's determination and eternal election, which is absolute and depending on the sovereign Will of God, and not on the free Will of man; as is evident from what has been said; and it being very evident from the Scriptures, that the eternal election which there is of saints to faith and holiness, is also an election of them to eternal salvation. Hence their appointment to salvation must also be absolute, and not depending on their contingent, self-determining Will. From all which it follows, that it is absolutely fixed in God's decree, that all true saints shall persevere to actual eternal salvation.

But I must leave all these things to the consideration of the fair and impartial reader; and when he has maturely weighed them, I would propose it to his consideration, whether many of the first reformers, and others that succeeded them, whom God in their day made the chief pillars of his church, and greatest instruments of their deliverance from error and darkness, and of the support of the cause of piety among them, have not been injured in the contempt with which they have been treated by many late writers, for their teaching and maintaining such doctrines as are commonly called *Calvinistic*. Indeed, some of these new writers, at the same time that they have represented the doctrines of these ancient and eminent divines as in the highest degree ridiculous, and contrary to common sense, in an ostentation of a very generous charity, have allowed that they were honest, well-meaning men; yea, it may be, some of them, as though it were in great condescension and compassion to them, have allowed that they did pretty well for the day in which they lived, and considering the great disadvantages they labored under; when at the same time, their manner of speaking has naturally and plainly suggested to the minds of their readers, that they were persons, who, through the lowness of their genius, and greatness of the bigotry with which their minds were shackled and thoughts confined, living in the gloomy caves of superstition, fondly embraced and demurely and zealously taught the most absurd, silly, and monstrous opinions, worthy of the greatest contempt of gentlemen possessed of that noble and generous freedom of thought, which happily prevails in this age of light and inquiry. When, indeed, such is the case, that we might, if so disposed, speak as big words as they, and on far better grounds. And really all the *Arminians* on earth might be challenged, without arrogance or vanity, to make these principles of theirs, wherein they mainly differ from their fathers, whom they so much despise, consistent with common sense; yea, and perhaps to produce any doctrine ever embraced by the blindest bigot of the church of Rome, or the most ignorant Mussulman or extravagant enthusiast, that might be reduced to more demonstrable inconsistencies, and repugnancies to common sense, and to themselves; though their inconsistencies indeed may not lie so deep, or be so artfully veiled by a deceitful ambiguity of words, and an indeterminate signification of phrases. I will not deny, that these gentlemen, many of them, are men of great abilities, and have been helped to higher attainments in philosophy, than those ancient divines, and have done great service to the church of God in some respects; but I humbly conceive that their differing from their fathers with such magisterial assurance, in these points in divinity, must be owing to some other cause than superior wisdom.

It may also be worthy of consideration, whether the great alteration, which has been made in the state of things in our nation, and some other parts of the Protestant world, in this and the past age, by the exploding so generally Calvinistic doctrines, that is so often spoken of as worthy to be greatly rejoiced in by the friends of truth, learning and virtue, as an instance of the great increase of light in the Christian church; I say, it may be worthy to be considered, whether this be indeed a happy change, owing to any such cause as an increase of true knowledge and understanding in things of religion; or whether there is not reason to fear, that it may be owing to some worse cause.

And I desire it may be considered, whether the boldness of some writers may not be worthy to be reflected on, who have not scrupled to say, that if these and those things are true (which yet appear to be the demonstrable dictates of reason, as well as the certain dictates of the mouth of the Most High) then God is unjust and cruel, and guilty of manifest deceit and double dealing and the like. Yea, some have gone so far, as confidently to assert, that if any book which pretends to be Scripture, teaches such doctrines, that alone is sufficient warrant for mankind to reject it, as what cannot be the word of God.—— Some, who have not gone so far, have said, that if the Scripture seems to teach any such doctrines, so contrary to reason, we are obliged to find out some other interpretation of those texts, where such doctrines seem to be exhibited. Others express themselves yet more modestly:

they express a tenderness and religious fear, lest they should receive and teach any thing that should seem to reflect on God's moral character, or be a disparagement to his methods of administration in his moral government; and therefore express themselves as not daring to embrace some doctrines, though they seem to be delivered in Scripture, according to the more obvious and natural construction of the words. But indeed it would show a truer modesty and humility, if they would more entirely rely on God's wisdom and discerning, who knows infinitely better than we, what is agreeable to his own perfections, and never intended to leave these matters to the decision of the wisdom and discerning of men; but by his own unerring instruction, to determine for us what the truth is; knowing how little our judgment is to be depended on, and how extremely prone vain and blind men are to err in such matters.

The truth of the case is, that if the Scripture plainly taught the opposite doctrines, to those that are so much stumbled at, viz., the *Arminian* doctrine of free Will, and others depending thereon, it would be the greatest of all difficulties that attend the Scriptures, incomparably greater than its containing any, even the most mysterious of those doctrines of the first reformers, which our late free-thinkers have so superciliously exploded.—Indeed, it is a glorious argument of the divinity of the holy Scriptures, that they teach such doctrines, which in one age and another, through the blindness of men's minds, and strong prejudices of their hearts, are rejected, as most absurd and unreasonable, by the wise and great men of the world; which yet, when they are most carefully and strictly examined, appear to be exactly agreeable to the most demonstrable, certain and natural dictates of reason. By such things it appears, that the *foolishness of God is wiser than men*, and God does as is said in 1 Cor. i. 19, 20: "For it is written, I will destroy the wisdom of the wise; I will bring to nothing the understanding of the prudent. Where is the wise? Where is the scribe? Where is the disputer of this world? Hath not God made foolish the wisdom of this world?" And as it used to be in time past, so it is probable it will be in time to come, as it is there written, in verses 27, 28, 29: "But God hath chosen the foolish things of the world, to confound the wise; and God hath chosen the weak things of the world, to confound the things that are mighty; and base things of the world, the things which are despised, hath God chosen: yea, and things which are not, to bring to nought things that are; that no flesh should glory in his presence." AMEN.

THE NATURE OF TRUE VIRTUE

Whatever controversies and variety of opinions there are about the nature of virtue, yet all (excepting some skeptics, who deny any real difference between virtue and vice) mean by it, something *beautiful*, or rather some kind of *beauty*, or excellency.—It is not *all* beauty, that is called virtue; for instance, not the beauty of a building, of a flower, or of the rainbow: but some beauty belonging to Beings that have *perception* and *will*.—It is not all beauty of *mankind*, that is called virtue; for instance, not the external beauty of the countenance, or shape, gracefulness of motion, or harmony of voice: but it is a beauty that has its original seat in the mind.—But yet perhaps not *every* thing that may be called a beauty of mind, is properly called virtue. There is a beauty of understanding and speculation. There is something in the ideas and conceptions of great philosophers and statesmen, that may be called beautiful; which is a different thing from what is most commonly meant by virtue. But virtue is the beauty of those qualities and acts of the mind, that are of a *moral* nature, i.e., such as are attended with desert or worthiness of *praise*, or *blame*. Things of this sort, it is generally agreed, so far as I know, are not any thing belonging merely to speculation; but to the *disposition* and *will*, or (to use a general word, I suppose commonly well understood) the *heart*. Therefore I suppose, I shall not depart from the common opinion, when I say, that virtue is the beauty of the qualities and exercises of the heart, or those actions which proceed from them. So that when it is inquired, What is the nature of true *virtue*?—this is the same as to inquire, what that is which renders any habit, disposition, or exercise of the heart truly *beautiful*. I use the phrase *true* virtue, and speak of things *truly* beautiful, because I suppose it will generally be allowed, that there is a distinction to be made between some things which are truly virtuous, and others which only seem to be virtuous, through a partial and imperfect view of things: that some actions and dispositions appear beautiful, if considered partially and superficially, or with regard to some things belonging to them, and in some of their circumstances and tendencies, which would appear otherwise in a more extensive and comprehensive view, wherein they are seen clearly in their whole nature and the extent of their connections in the universality of things.—There is a general and a particular beauty. By a *particular* beauty, I mean that by which a thing appears beautiful when considered only with regard to its connection with, and tendency to some particular things within a limited, and, as it were, a private sphere. And a *general* beauty is that by which a thing appears beautiful when viewed most perfectly, comprehensively and universally, with regard to all its tendencies, and its connections with every thing it stands related to. The former may be without and against the latter. As, a few notes in a tune, taken only by themselves, and in their relation to one another, may be harmonious; which when considered with respect to all the notes in the tune, or the entire series of sounds they are connected with, may be very discordant and disagreeable.—(Of which more afterwards.)—*That only*, therefore, is what I mean by true virtue, which is *that*, belonging to the *heart* of an intelligent Being, that is beautiful by a *general* beauty, or beautiful in a comprehensive view as it is in itself, and as related to every thing that it stands in connection with. And therefore when we are inquiring concerning the nature of true virtue, viz., wherein this true and general beauty of the heart does most essentially consist—this is my answer to the inquiry:

True virtue most essentially consists in benevolence to Being in general. Or perhaps to speak more accurately, it is that consent, propensity and union of heart to Being in general, that is immediately exercised in a general good will.

The things which were before observed of the nature of true virtue, naturally lead us to such a notion of it. If it has its seat in the heart, and is the general goodness and beauty of the disposition and exercise of that, in the most comprehensive view, considered with regard to its universal tendency, and as related to every thing that it stands in connection with; what can it consist in, but a consent and good will to Being in general?—Beauty does not consist in discord and dissent, but in consent and agreement. And if every intelligent Being is some way related to Being in general, and is a part of the universal system of existence; and so stands in connection with the whole; what can its general and true beauty be, but its union and consent with the great whole?

If any such thing can be supposed as a union of heart to some particular Being, or number of Beings, disposing it to benevolence to a private circle or system of Beings, which are but a small part of the whole; not implying a tendency to a union with the great system, and not at all inconsistent with enmity towards Being in general; this I suppose not to be of the nature of true virtue: although it may in some respects be good, and may appear beautiful in a confined and contracted view of things.—But of this more afterwards.

It is abundantly plain by the holy Scriptures, and generally allowed, not only by Christian divines, but by the more considerable deists, that virtue most essentially consists in love. And I suppose, it is owned by the most considerable writers, to consist in general love of benevolence, or kind affection: though it seems to me, the meaning of some in this affair is not sufficiently explained, which perhaps occasions some error or confusion in discourses on this subject.

When I say, true virtue consists in love to Being in general, I shall not be likely to be understood, that no one act of the mind or exercise of love is of the nature of true virtue, but what has Being in general, or the great system of universal existence, for its direct and immediate object: so that no exercise of love or kind affection to any one particular Being, that is but a small part of this whole, has any thing of the nature of true virtue. But, that the nature of true virtue consists in a disposition to benevolence towards Being in general. Though, from such a disposition may arise exercises of love to particular Beings, as objects are presented and occasions arise. No wonder, that he who is of a generally benevolent disposition, should be more disposed than another to have his heart moved with benevolent affection to particular persons, whom he is acquainted and conversant with, and from whom arise the greatest and most frequent occasions for exciting his benevolent temper. But my meaning is, that no affections towards particular persons or Beings are of the nature of true virtue, but such as arise from a generally benevolent temper, or from that habit or frame of mind, wherein consists a disposition to love Being in general.

And perhaps it is needless for me to give notice to my readers, that when I speak of an intelligent Being's having a heart united and benevolently disposed to Being in general, I thereby mean *intelligent* Being in general. Not inanimate things, or Beings that have no perception or will, which are not properly capable objects of benevolence.

Love is commonly distinguished into love of benevolence and love of complacence. Love of *benevolence* is that affection or propensity of the heart to any Being, which causes it to incline to its well being, or disposes it to desire and take pleasure in its happiness. And if I mistake not, it is agreeable to the common opinion, that beauty in the object is not always the ground of this propensity: but that there may be such a thing as benevolence, or a disposition to the welfare of those that are not considered as beautiful; unless mere existence be accounted a beauty. And benevolence or goodness in the Divine Being is generally supposed, not only to be prior to the beauty of many of its objects, but to their existence: so as to be the ground both of their existence and their beauty, rather than they the foundation of God's benevolence; as it is supposed that it is God's goodness which moved him to give them both Being and beauty. So that if all virtue primarily consists in that affection of heart to Being, which is exercised in benevolence, or an inclination to its good, then God's virtue is so extended as to include a propensity, not only to Being actually existing, and actually beautiful, but to possible Being, so as to incline him to give Being, beauty and happiness. But not now to insist particularly on this. What I would have observed at present, is, that it must be allowed, benevolence doth not necessarily presuppose beauty in its object.

What is commonly called love of *complacence*, presupposes beauty. For it is no other than delight in beauty; or complacence in the person or Being beloved for his beauty.

If virtue be the beauty of an intelligent Being, and virtue consists in love, then it is a plain inconsistence, to suppose that virtue primarily consists in any love to its object *for its beauty*; either in a love of complacence, which is delight in a Being for his beauty, or in a love of benevolence, that has the beauty of its object for its foundation. For that would be to suppose, that the beauty of intelligent Beings primarily consists in love to beauty;

or, that their virtue first of all consists in their love to virtue. Which is an inconsistence, and going in a circle. Because it makes virtue, or beauty of mind, the foundation or first motive of that love wherein virtue originally consists, or wherein the very first virtue consists; or, it supposes the first virtue to be the consequence and effect of virtue. So that virtue is originally the foundation and exciting cause of the very beginning or first Being of virtue. Which makes the first virtue, both the ground, and the consequence, both cause and effect of itself. Doubtless virtue primarily consists in something else besides any effect or consequence of virtue. If virtue consists primarily in love to virtue, then virtue, the thing loved, is the love of virtue: so that virtue must consist in the love of the love of virtue. And if it be inquired, what that virtue is, which virtue consists in the love of the love of, it must be answered, it is the love of virtue. So that there must be the love of the love of the love of virtue, and so on *ad infinitum*. For there is no end of going back in a circle. We never come to any beginning, or foundation. For it is without beginning and hangs on nothing.

Therefore if the essence of virtue or beauty of mind lies in love, or a disposition to love, it must primarily consist in something *different* both from complacence, which is a delight in beauty, and also from any benevolence that has the beauty of its object for its foundation. Because it is absurd, to say that virtue is primarily and first of all the consequence of itself. For this makes virtue primarily prior to itself.

Nor can virtue primarily consist in *gratitude*; or one Being's benevolence to another for his benevolence to him. Because this implies the same inconsistence. For it supposes a benevolence prior to gratitude, that is the cause of gratitude. Therefore the first benevolence, or that benevolence which has none prior to it, cannot be gratitude.

Therefore there is room left for no other conclusion than that the primary object of virtuous love is Being, simply considered; or, that true virtue primarily consists, not in love to any particular Beings, because of their virtue or beauty, nor in gratitude, because they love us; but in a propensity and union of heart to Being simply considered; exciting absolute benevolence (if I may so call it) to Being in general.—I say, true virtue *primarily* consists in this. For I am far from asserting that there is no true virtue in any other love than this absolute benevolence. But I would express what appears to me to be the truth on this subject, in the following particulars.

The *first* object of a virtuous benevolence is *Being*, simply considered: and if Being, *simply* considered, be its object, then Being *in general* is its object; and the thing it has an ultimate propensity to, is the *highest good* of Being in general. And it will seek the good of every *individual* Being unless it be conceived as not consistent with the highest good of Being in general. In which case the good of a particular Being, or some Beings, may be given up for the sake of the highest good of Being in general. And particularly if there be any Being that is looked upon as statedly and irreclaimably opposite and an enemy to Being in general, then consent and adherence to Being in general will induce the truly virtuous heart to forsake that Being, and to oppose it.

And further, if Being simply considered, be the first object of a truly virtuous benevolence, then that Being who has *most* of Being, or has the greatest share of existence, other things being equal, so far as such a Being is exhibited to our faculties or set in our view, will have the *greatest* share of the propensity and benevolent affection of the heart. I say, *other things being equal*, especially because there is a *secondary* object of virtuous benevolence, that I shall take notice of presently. Which is one thing that must be considered as the ground or motive to a purely virtuous benevolence. Pure benevolence in its first exercise is nothing else but Being's uniting consent, or propensity to Being; appearing true and pure by its extending to Being in general, and inclining to the general highest good, and to each Being, whose welfare is consistent with the highest general good, in proportion to the degree of *existence* understood, other things being equal.

The *second* object of a virtuous propensity of heart is *benevolent* Being. A secondary ground of pure benevolence is virtuous benevolence itself in its object. When any one under the influence of general benevolence, sees another Being possessed of the like general benevolence, this attaches his heart to him, and draws forth greater love to him, than merely his having existence: because so far as the Being beloved has love to Being in general, so far his own Being is, as it were, enlarged, extends to, and in some sort comprehends, Being in general: and therefore he that is governed by love to Being in general must of necessity have complacence in him, and the greater degree of benevolence to him, as it were out of gratitude to him for his love to general existence, that his own heart is extended and united to, and so looks on its interest as its own. It is because his heart is thus united to Being in general, that he looks on a benevolent propensity to Being in general, wherever he sees it, as the beauty of the Being in whom it is; an excellency, that renders him worthy of esteem, complacence, and the greater good will.

But several things may be noted more particularly concerning this secondary ground of a truly virtuous love.

1. That loving a Being on *this ground* necessarily arises from pure benevolence to Being *in general*, and comes to the same thing. For he that has a simple and pure good will to general entity or existence, must love that temper in others, that agrees and conspires with itself. A spirit

of consent to Being must agree with consent to Being. That which truly and sincerely seeks the good of others, must approve of, and love, that which joins with him in seeking the good of others.

2. This which has been now mentioned as a secondary ground of virtuous love, is the thing wherein true moral or spiritual *beauty* primarily consists. Yea, spiritual beauty consists wholly in this, and the various qualities and exercises of mind which proceed from it, and the external actions which proceed from these internal qualities and exercises. And in these things consists all true *virtue*, viz., in this love of Being, and the qualities and acts which arise from it.

3. As all spiritual beauty lies in these virtuous principles and acts, so it is primarily *on this account* they are beautiful, *viz.*, that they imply *consent* and *union* with Being *in general*. This is the primary and most essential Beauty of every thing that can justly be called by the name of virtue, or is any moral excellency in the eye of one that has a perfect view of things. I say, the *primary* and *most essential* beauty—because there is a secondary and inferior sort of beauty; which I shall take notice of afterwards.

4. This spiritual beauty, that is but a *secondary* ground of a virtuous benevolence, is the ground, not only of benevolence, but *complacence*, and is the *primary* ground of the latter; that is, when the complacence is truly virtuous. Love to us in particular, and kindness received, may be a secondary ground. But this is the primary objective foundation of it.

5. It must be noted, that the *degree* of the *amiableness* or *valuableness* of true virtue, primarily consisting in consent and a benevolent propensity of heart to Being in general, in the eyes of one that is influenced by such a spirit, is not in the *simple* proportion of the degree of benevolent affection seen, but in a proportion *com-*

pounded of the greatness of the benevolent Being or the degree of *Being* and the degree of *benevolence.* One that loves Being in general, will necessarily value good will to Being in general, wherever he sees it. But if he sees the same benevolence in *two* Beings, he will value it *more* in two, than in one only. Because it is a greater thing, more favorable to Being in general, to have two Beings to favor it, than only one of them. For there is more Being that favors Being: both together having more Being than one alone. So, if one Being be as great as two, has as much existence as both together, and has the same degree of general benevolence, it is more favorable to Being in general than if there were general benevolence in a Being that had but half that share of existence. As a large quantity of gold, with the same degree of preciousness, i.e., with the same excellent quality of matter, is more valuable than a small quantity of the same metal.

6. It is impossible that any one should truly *relish* this beauty, consisting in general benevolence, who has *not* that temper himself. I have observed, that if any Being is possessed of such a temper, he will unavoidably be pleased with the same temper in another. And it may in like manner be demonstrated, that it is such a spirit, and nothing else, which will relish such a spirit. For if a Being, destitute of benevolence, should love benevolence to Being in general, it would prize and seek that which it had no value for. Because to love an inclination to the good of Being in general, would imply a loving and prizing the good of Being in general. For how should one love and value a *disposition* to a thing, or a *tendency to promote* a thing, and for that very reason, because it tends to promote it—when the *thing* itself is what he is regardless of, and has no value for, nor desires to have promoted. . . .